completely
breakfast

ISBN: 978-1-59955-102-9

Published by CFI, an imprint of Cedar Fort, Inc., 2373 W. 700 S., Springville, UT 84663
Distributed by Cedar Fort, Inc., www.cedarfort.com

LIBRARY OF CONGRESS CATALOGING-IN-PUBLICATION DATA

Duda, Carlene, 1962–
   Completely breakfast / Carlene Duda.
      p. cm.
   Includes bibliographical references and index.
   ISBN 978-1-59955-102-9 (alk. paper)
   1. Breakfasts. I. Title.

   TX733.D843 2008
   642—dc22

                    2008009863

Cover by Nicole Williams
Editing and page design by Lyndsee Simpson Cordes
Cover design © 2008 by Lyle Mortimer

Printed in China

10 9 8 7 6 5 4 3 2

Printed on acid-free paper

completely breakfast

Carlene Duda

CFI
Springville, Utah

No day is complete without breakfast!

With today's hectic schedules, finding the time to prepare breakfast can be challenging. Here are some tips for making this important meal a little easier to get on the table.

Don't think of berries as an extravagance. They are outrageously good for you. They turn the most boring bowl of cereal into something special and a stack of pancakes into a majestic mountain.

Always keep a bowl of fresh seasonal fruits available for the easiest grab-and-go.

Keep hard-boiled eggs in your fridge—it's an easy dose of high-quality protein.

Set foods aside the night before. Cut up fruits, pour cereal, or prepare mixtures for baked or scrambled eggs in advance.

Breakfast in French, *petit déjeuner*, literally translates to "small lunch," a good thing to keep in mind when including food groups.

contents

breakfast casseroles

Victorian Breakfast Casserole

Cracker Barrel Casserole

Christmas Breakfast Casserole

Baked Eggs with Canadian Bacon

Six-Layer Breakfast Casserole

Overnight Bacon Casserole

Amish Breakfast Casserole

Sausage Brunch Casserole

Green-Pepper Egg Puff

Breakfast Sausage Pie

Northwest Breakfast Casserole

Baked French Toast Casserole

Northwest Breakfast Casserole, page 14

Breakfast Casserole Tips

If you are planning a family gathering, prepare the casserole, serve it with a bowl of fresh fruit and slices of toast, and let everyone dig in.

Preparation is as simple as turning the dial on the oven and letting breakfast bake itself.

You can assemble the casserole in advance so that by the time morning rolls around there is minimal time spent on kitchen duty. The prep work will pay off—these comforting dishes are crowd pleasers.

Victorian Breakfast Casserole

No more hurried mornings! Make this casserole and refrigerate.
In the morning you are ready to bake, relax, and enjoy!

12 slices white bread, crusts
removed
12 ham slices
1 cup shredded sharp cheddar
cheese
¼ cup chopped onion
¼ cup chopped green pepper
6 eggs
3 cups milk
½ tsp. salt
½ tsp. pepper
1 tsp. mustard
½ tsp. Worcestershire sauce
½ cup butter, melted
2 cups crushed cornflakes

Grease a 9x13-inch baking pan.

Layer pan starting with six slices of bread, six ham slices, and ½ cup cheese; repeat layering. Spread chopped onions and green peppers on top.

In a medium bowl, beat together eggs, milk, salt, pepper, mustard, and Worcestershire sauce. Pour mixture over bread layers.

Cover and refrigerate overnight.

Preheat oven to 350 degrees.

Before baking, remove cover, pour melted butter over casserole, and sprinkle crushed cornflakes on top. Bake for 1 hour. Let stand 10 minutes before serving.

Makes 12 servings.

Cracker Barrel Casserole

A tasty egg-bake made with crackers and cheese.

¼ cup + 2 Tbsp. butter, divided
2 medium onions, chopped
2 cups shredded Swiss cheese,
    divided
1 cup crushed saltine crackers,
    divided
2 eggs
¼ cup evaporated milk
1 tsp. salt
½ tsp. pepper

Bake 25 minutes at 350 degrees.

Melt ¼ cup butter in large skillet over medium heat.

Add onions and sauté until tender. Place half of the onions in the bottom of a 1½-quart deep-dish pie pan.

Sprinkle 1 cup Swiss cheese and ½ cup cracker crumbs over the onions. Layer the remaining onions and cheese.

In a medium-size bowl, beat eggs, milk, salt, and pepper. Pour mixture evenly over onion layers. Melt 2 tablespoons butter in skillet over medium heat; stir in remaining cracker crumbs, lightly browning, and then sprinkle crumbs over casserole.

Christmas Breakfast Casserole

When it's time to string the lights, it's time to gather friends and enjoy time together.

1 pound sausage links

4–5 slices sourdough bread,
   cubed

2 cups shredded cheddar
   cheese

5 eggs

¾ tsp. dry mustard

2¼ + ⅔ cups milk

1 (10.75-oz.) can cream of
   mushroom soup

Brown, drain, and cut sausage links into ½-inch rounds. Grease a 9x13-inch baking dish. Scatter bread cubes in bottom of baking dish. Top with cheese and sausage. Set aside.

Whisk together eggs, mustard, and 2¼ cups milk in a small mixing bowl. Pour over bread/cheese/sausage mixture. Cover and refrigerate overnight.

Preheat oven to 300 degrees. Dilute mushroom soup with ⅔ cup milk. Pour over casserole.

Bake 1 hour, uncovered. Serve hot from the oven.

Baked Eggs with Canadian Bacon

This is one of the easiest ways to impress a crowd. Great for guests or an early brunch!

4 eggs
1 cup milk
2 Tbsp. butter
¼ cup chopped mushrooms
¼ cup chopped green bell
 peppers
¼ cup chopped onion
4 slices Canadian bacon
paprika

Preheat oven to 325 degrees. In a large bowl, mix together eggs and milk; beat until frothy.

Melt butter in a skillet over low heat. Sauté mushrooms, peppers, and onions until limp. Stir sautéed vegetables into egg mixture and pour into a buttered 8x8-inch baking pan. Place slices of Canadian bacon on top of the egg mixture. Sprinkle with paprika.

Bake 20 minutes, uncovered, or until eggs are set.

Six-Layer Breakfast Casserole

This casserole is perfect to double for a large family or for company.
It reheats great in the microwave for the next day.

6 eggs
¼ cup heavy cream
¼ tsp. pepper
1 tsp. salt
1 pound ground sausage,
    cooked and crumbled
¼ cup jalapenos, cut in ¼-inch
    slices (optional)
½ cup shredded cheddar
    cheese
1 tsp. garlic
1 tsp. ground cumin
3 slices thick bread

Preheat oven to 350 degrees. Grease the bottom of a 2-quart baking dish. Set aside.

In a medium-size bowl, combine eggs, cream, pepper, and salt. Beat well until blended.

In a separate bowl, combine cooked sausage, jalapenos, cheese, garlic, and cumin.

To assemble, place one-third of the egg mixture in the bottom of prepared pan. Place 1 slice of bread on top. Spread one-third of the sausage mixture over the bread.

Continue layering, ending with sausage on top. Bake 15 minutes or until eggs are set.

Makes 4 servings.

Overnight Bacon Casserole

Perfect for holiday overnight guests or a brunch, this one features bacon and cheddar cheese. You won't have any leftovers.

1 pound sliced bacon
8 slices whole wheat bread
6 eggs
1½ cup milk
1 cup shredded cheddar
   cheese
½ tsp. dry mustard

Grease an 8x8-inch baking pan. Cut strips of bacon crosswise into ½-inch pieces. Cook in skillet over medium heat until crisp. Drain off excess fat.

Remove crusts from bread. Cut into cubes; set aside.

In a large bowl, beat eggs. Stir in milk, cheese, mustard, and bacon. Gently stir in bread cubes. Spoon into prepared baking dish. Cover tightly and refrigerate overnight.

Remove from refrigerator and let stand at room temperature for 15 minutes.

Bake, uncovered, 45–50 minutes at 350 degrees.

Amish Breakfast Casserole

This tried-and-true casserole will bring warmth and tradition to your table.

---

1 pound bacon, diced
1 medium onion, chopped
6 eggs, beaten
4 cups shredded hash browns
2 cups shredded cheddar
   cheese
1½ cup cottage cheese
1¼ cup shredded Swiss cheese

In a large skillet, cook bacon and onion until bacon is crisp. Drain.

Mix the remaining ingredients and add to bacon mixture. Pour into a greased 9x13-inch pan.

Bake, uncovered, at 350 degrees for 35–40 minutes or until eggs are set and bubbly. Let stand 10 minutes before serving.

Makes 8–10 servings.

Sausage Brunch Casserole

Ease meets flavor!
Time is of the essence with this easy egg-and-cheese casserole.

10 eggs, beaten
⅓ cup flour
¾ cup baking powder
10 ounces ground sausage,
    cooked and crumbled
1 cup shredded Monterey Jack
    cheese
1½ cup cottage cheese

Preheat oven to 375 degrees.

Mix the eggs, flour, and baking powder well. Add the sausage, cheese, and cottage cheese. Beat well.

Pour into a greased 9x13-inch glass baking dish. Bake 30–35 minutes.

Makes 4–6 servings.

Green-Pepper Egg Puff

Fresh seasonal peppers will lend both color and taste to this egg puff.

1 large green pepper, chopped
1 cup shredded Monterey Jack
   cheese
1 cup shredded cheddar
   cheese
8 eggs
1 cup milk
2 Tbsp. flour
dash of salt
salsa
sour cream

Preheat oven to 350 degrees.

Evenly distribute chopped green peppers in the bottom of an ungreased 8x8-inch baking dish. Cover with cheeses.

Whisk together eggs, milk, flour, and salt; pour over cheeses.

Bake 40 minutes. Serve with salsa and sour cream.

Breakfast Sausage Pie

Relatives, friends, and the guest of honor will enjoy this fresh spring luncheon.
You'll surely enjoy its ease!

1 (9-inch) deep-dish pie shell

1½ cup shredded mozzarella
    cheese, divided

1 pound ground sausage,
    cooked and crumbled

4 eggs

¾ cup milk

Line pie shell with ¾ cup cheese. Cover with cooked sausage. Top with remaining cheese. Mix eggs and milk, and pour over cheese.

Bake at 325 degrees for approximately 40 minutes or until set.

Makes 8 servings.

Northwest Breakfast Casserole

This casserole is hearty and fulfilling—
a Northwest classic with potatoes and Johnny's seasoning salt.

12 eggs
1 cup plain yogurt
1 tsp. Johnny's seasoning salt
¾ stick butter
¼ cup chopped onion
2 cups shredded hash browns
1 cup shredded sharp cheddar
cheese

Preheat oven to 350 degrees. Beat eggs, yogurt, and seasoning salt together. In large skillet, melt butter and lightly sauté onion. Add hash browns; stir to mix. Pour in egg mixture; stir just until mixed.

Pour into casserole dish. Sprinkle shredded cheese over casserole. Bake approximately 25 minutes or until set (when a knife inserted in center comes out clean). Cut into 8 squares.

Baked French Toast Casserole

Turn breakfast into a five-star affair.
This French toast is rather rich. You deserve it!

French toast:

1 loaf French bread
8 large eggs
2 cups half-and-half
1 cup milk
2 Tbsp. sugar
1 Tbsp. vanilla
½ tsp. nutmeg
½ tsp. cinnamon
dash of salt

Praline topping:

1 cup butter, softened
1 cup brown sugar
1 cup chopped pecans
2 Tbsp. corn syrup
½ tsp. cinnamon
½ tsp. nutmeg

Slice French bread into 20 slices, 1-inch thick each.

Arrange slices on a generously buttered cookie sheet in 2 rows, overlapping the slices.

In a large bowl, combine the eggs, half-and-half, milk, sugar, vanilla, nutmeg, cinnamon, and salt. Whisk until blended.

Pour mixture over the bread slices, making sure they are covered evenly with the egg mixture. Spoon some of the mixture between the slices. Cover with foil and refrigerate overnight.

The next day, preheat oven to 350 degrees.

Prepare praline topping by combining all ingredients in a medium bowl and mixing well. Spread topping evenly over the bread.

Bake 45 minutes or until puffed and lightly golden. Serve with warm raspberry jam.

quiche & frittatas

Individual Quiche

Parmesan and Herb Frittata

Sun-Dried Tomato Frittata

Frittata with Asparagus and Ham

Bacon Cheddar Frittata

Bacon and Cheese Crustless Quiche

Pesto and Provolone Quiche

Tomato Spinach Frittata

Parmesan Basil Breakfast Strata

Mini Potato and Bacon Frittatas

Bacon and Cheese Crustless Quiche, page 25

Pesto and Provolone Quiche, page 26

Quiche and Frittata Tips

A frittata is basically an unfolded omelet. You can add almost any vegetable, cheese, or meat. Frittatas are served in wedges.

Quiche is a wonderfully easy, versatile dish that can be eaten at any time of the day. It is a custard-like dish—the eggs are mixed with cream—and is usually baked in a pie or tart crust.

Want to make a quiche even easier? If you don't have the time to make your quiche crust from scratch, use a frozen pre-made crust.

Use whole milk or cream when possible. Watery milk will leave you with a watery quiche that you might overbake because you think it's not done in the middle.

If you have a pizza stone, bake your quiche on it. This will ensure the crust is baked through and not soggy.

Individual Quiche

Extraordinary made easy, using toaster waffles as a quick and tasty base.

6 toaster waffles, toasted
cooking spray
1 cup shredded Swiss cheese
½ cup cooked and crumbled
  bacon
2 eggs
½ cup plain yogurt
2 Tbsp. sliced green onion
¼ tsp. salt
¼ tsp. garlic powder
¼ tsp. pepper

Preheat oven to 350 degrees. Place toasted waffles on a foil-lined cookie sheet coated with cooking spray.

Sprinkle each waffle with cheese and bacon. In a medium bowl, combine eggs, yogurt, green onions, salt, garlic powder, and pepper. Spread evenly over the waffles.

Bake 25 minutes or until set and lightly browned. Serve hot.

Makes 6 servings.

Parmesan and Herb Frittata

This frittata cooks first on the stovetop and then in the oven.
Be sure that your skillet has an oven-safe handle.

6 eggs, lightly beaten

½ cup shredded Parmesan
cheese

¼ tsp. salt

¼ tsp. pepper

1 Tbsp. olive oil

¼ cup finely chopped onion

2 Tbsp. minced parsley

Preheat oven to 350 degrees. In a medium-size bowl, whisk together eggs, Parmesan cheese, salt, and pepper.

Heat the oil in a 10-inch nonstick ovenproof skillet over medium heat.

Add the onions and cook until softened. Add parsley and egg mixture, stirring gently until the eggs on the bottom are firmly set. Gently pull the cooked eggs back from one edge of the skillet and tilt the pan, allowing any uncooked egg to run to the cleared edge of the skillet. Repeat this process, working your way around the skillet, until the egg on top is mostly set but still moist, 1–2 minutes.

Transfer the skillet to the oven and bake until the frittata edges are set and dry to the touch, about 3 minutes. Run a spatula around the skillet edge to loosen the frittata. Invert it onto a serving plate. Serve warm.

Sun-Dried Tomato Frittata

Deep, simple, and satisfying, these flavors are music to your ears.

6 eggs, lightly beaten

½ cup shredded mozzarella
    cheese

¼ tsp. salt

¼ tsp. pepper

1 Tbsp. olive oil

¼ cup finely chopped onion

2 Tbsp. fresh basil, minced

¼ cup oil-packed sun-dried
    tomatoes, drained

Preheat oven to 350 degrees.

In a medium-size bowl, whisk together eggs, mozzarella, salt, and pepper.

Heat the oil over medium heat in a 10-inch nonstick ovenproof skillet. Add the onions and cook until softened. Add basil, tomatoes, and egg mixture. Stir gently until the eggs on the bottom are set and firm. Gently pull the cooked eggs back from one edge of the skillet and tilt the pan, allowing any uncooked egg to run to the cleared edge of the skillet. Repeat this process, working your way around the skillet, until the egg on top is mostly set but still moist, 1–2 minutes.

Transfer the skillet to the oven and bake until the frittata edge is set and dry to the touch, about 3 minutes. Run a spatula around the skillet edge to loosen the frittata. Invert it onto a serving plate. Serve warm.

Frittata with Asparagus and Ham

One quick trip to the summer farmers' market and you'll have all you'll need for this fresh frittata.

½ pound asparagus

6 eggs, lightly beaten

½ cup shredded Monterey Jack
   cheese

¼ tsp. salt

¼ tsp. pepper

1 Tbsp. olive oil

¼ cup finely chopped onion

¼ cup ham

2 Tbsp. parsley

Preheat oven to 350 degrees. Trim off tough ends of asparagus and cut into ¼-inch pieces.

In a medium-size bowl, whisk together eggs, Monterey Jack cheese, salt, and pepper.

Heat the oil over medium heat in a 10-inch nonstick ovenproof skillet. Add the onions and asparagus and cook until softened; add ham. Stir. Add parsley and egg mixture. Stir gently until the eggs on the bottom are set and firm.

Gently pull the cooked eggs back from one edge of the skillet and tilt the pan, allowing any uncooked egg to run to the cleared edge of the skillet. Repeat this process, working your way around the skillet, until the egg on top is mostly set but still moist, 1–2 minutes.

Transfer the skillet to the oven and bake until the frittata edge is set and dry to the touch, about 3 minutes. Run a spatula around the skillet edge to loosen the frittata. Invert it onto a serving plate. Serve warm.

Bacon Cheddar Frittata

*The classic frittata offers an excellent last-minute solution
for those times when you don't have a lot of ingredients in the fridge.*

3 eggs
½ cup milk
1 green onion, chopped
1 Tbsp. butter, melted
¼ tsp. salt
dash of pepper
½ cup shredded cheddar
   cheese
1 slice bacon, cooked and
   crumbled

Preheat oven to 400 degrees.

In a bowl, whisk the eggs, milk, onion, butter, salt, and pepper. Pour into a shallow 3-cup baking dish coated with nonstick cooking spray. Sprinkle with cheese and bacon.

Bake, uncovered, for 12–15 minutes or until eggs are set.

Makes 2 servings.

Bacon and Cheese Crustless Quiche

No more soggy crusts!

1 cup sliced green onion,
    divided
1 cup chopped tomatoes,
    divided
12 slices bacon
1 cup sliced fresh mushrooms
12 eggs
⅓ cup sour cream
1 cup shredded cheddar
    cheese
1 cup shredded mozzarella
    cheese

Preheat oven to 325 degrees. Reserve 2 tablespoons each of onions and tomatoes; set aside for topping.

Cook bacon in large skillet until crisp. Remove bacon and drain on paper towels. Reserve 1 tablespoon of the bacon drippings in the skillet. Chop bacon.

Add chopped bacon and mushrooms to skillet. Cook and stir until tender, about 2 minutes. Remove from heat. Add green onions and tomatoes, mixing well.

Beat eggs and sour cream with a wire whisk until well blended. Pour into a greased 9x13-inch baking dish and top with the bacon mixture and cheeses.

Bake 30 minutes or until center is set (when a knife inserted in center comes out clean). Sprinkle with reserved onions and tomatoes. Let stand 5 minutes before cutting into pieces.

Makes 12 servings.

Pesto and Provolone Quiche

*Baking the crust slightly before adding the filling helps ensure
that it cooks thoroughly and will not be soggy.*

1 refrigerated pie crust

2 cups shredded Provolone
cheese, divided

3 Tbsp. refrigerated pesto

¼ cup shredded Parmesan
cheese

½ cup chopped red bell pepper

5 eggs

1½ cup milk

¼ tsp. salt

Preheat oven to 425 degrees.

Place pie crust in a 9-inch glass pie plate.
Bake 7 minutes.

Remove crust from oven. Sprinkle 1 cup
Provolone cheese over bottom of crust.

In a small bowl, mix pesto and Parmesan
cheese until smooth. Carefully spread over
Provolone cheese. Sprinkle with bell pepper and remaining Provolone cheese.

In a medium bowl, beat eggs, milk, and
salt until well blended. Pour over cheese.

Bake 7 minutes. Reduce oven temperature to 325 degrees; bake 15 minutes.

Cover edge of crust with foil. Bake 25–30
minutes longer or until set (when a knife
inserted in the center comes out clean). Let
stand 5 minutes before serving.

Tomato Spinach Frittata

The tomato and spinach create a festival of colors and flavors!

6 eggs

⅓ cup shredded Parmesan cheese

½ tsp. basil

½ tsp. garlic powder

⅛ tsp. nutmeg

¼ tsp. salt

¼ tsp. pepper

2 tsp. olive oil

6 cups spinach, loosely packed

6 cherry tomatoes, quartered

In a small bowl, beat eggs with wire whisk. Stir in cheese, basil, garlic powder, nutmeg, salt, and pepper; set aside.

Heat oil over medium heat in a 10-inch nonstick skillet with sloping sides. Add spinach; cover and cook 2–3 minutes, until spinach is slightly wilted. Stir occasionally and watch carefully to prevent burning. Add 1–2 tablespoons of water if spinach becomes dry.

Reduce heat to low. Spread spinach evenly in skillet; top with tomatoes. Pour egg mixture over top. Cover; cook 12–15 minutes or until bottom is lightly browned and top is set, lifting edges occasionally to allow uncooked egg mixture to flow to bottom of skillet. Cut into wedges and serve.

Makes 6 servings.

Parmesan Basil Breakfast Strata

This dish has a more subtle flavor.
It's a perfect blend to please any palate.

6 eggs
3½ cups milk
1 Tbsp. minced onion
1 tsp. salt
½ tsp. pepper
8 cups French bread, cut into
   1-inch cubes
2 cups shredded mozzarella
   cheese
¼ cup pesto
½ cup shredded Parmesan
   cheese

In a large bowl, beat eggs with wire whisk until foamy. Beat in milk, onions, salt, and pepper. Set aside.

Spray a 9x13-inch baking dish with cooking spray. Place bread cubes in bottom of baking dish. Sprinkle with mozzarella cheese. Pour egg mixture over top. Swirl pesto through mixture with a spoon. Sprinkle Parmesan cheese over top.

Cover with plastic wrap. Refrigerate 8 hours or overnight.

Heat oven to 350 degrees. Bake, uncovered, 40–45 minutes or until set (when a knife inserted in center comes out clean). Let stand 5–10 minutes before serving.

Mini Potato and Bacon Frittatas

These mini frittatas are great for any brunch or breakfast on the go. If you don't have a mini muffin pan, you can cook the frittata in a 9x13-inch pan for 15 minutes and simply cut into 36 squares.

2 cups peeled, finely chopped
  potato
6 slices bacon, uncooked
½ cup chopped onion
1 tsp. salt, divided
¼ tsp. thyme
½ cup chopped fresh chives,
  divided
2 Tbsp. shredded Parmesan
  cheese
¼ tsp. pepper
3 eggs, beaten
7 egg whites
⅓ cup sour cream

Preheat oven to 375 degrees. Place chopped potatoes in a medium-size saucepan and cover with water. Bring to a boil and cook 3 minutes, until almost tender. Drain.

Cook bacon in a large nonstick skillet over medium heat until crisp. Remove bacon from pan, crumble, and set aside. Discard bacon drippings, leaving 2 tablespoons in pan. Add potatoes, onions, ¼ teaspoon salt, and thyme to pan. Cook 8 minutes or until potatoes are lightly brown. Remove from heat and cool.

Whisk together the potato mixture, bacon, remaining ¾ teaspoon salt, 2 tablespoons chives, cheese, pepper, eggs, and egg whites.

Spray 36 mini muffins cups with cooking spray. Spoon about 1 tablespoon egg mixture into each muffin cup.

Bake 16 minutes or until light brown. Cool 5 minutes on a wire rack. Remove frittatas from muffin cups.

Top each mini frittata with 1 teaspoon sour cream and a sprinkle of chives.

skillets

Ham Potato Skillet

Patches of Potatoes

Savory Fried Potatoes

Campfire Breakfast Skillet

Breakfast Fried Potatoes

Breakfast Fried Potatoes, page 38

Skillet Tips

When making a skillet dish, use the correct cooking skillet for the job. Nonstick skillets are absolutely necessary for scrambled eggs, pancakes, and crepes. They are also best for cooking with very little fat, or for cooking recipes that have lots of liquid.

Heavy skillets, like those made from stainless steel or cast iron, are best for browning and creating crusts on foods. General uses are searing, sautéing, and stir-frying meats and vegetables. One limitation is that you cannot cook completely fat-free—some oil must be added to the pan because delicate foods tend to stick.

Never put a cast-iron skillet in the dishwasher.

Ham Potato Skillet

In many areas, gardeners can grow these fresh ingredients right in their backyard.
Using leftover ham from the night before, you've got the perfect summer breakfast.

4 tsp. butter

3 medium potatoes, peeled and
thinly sliced

2 green onions, chopped

⅓ cup chopped yellow onion

2 cups cooked, diced ham

½ tsp. salt

¼ tsp. pepper

3 eggs, lightly beaten

½ cup shredded cheddar
cheese

½ cup shredded Monterey Jack
cheese

chopped fresh parsley

In a 10-inch skillet, melt butter over medium heat. In the same skillet, layer potatoes, onions, ham, salt, and pepper. Cover and cook over medium heat for 10–15 minutes or until potatoes are tender.

Pour eggs over the top. Cover and cook 3–5 minutes or until eggs are nearly set. Uncover and sprinkle cheeses on top.

Replace cover and cook 3–5 minutes longer, until cheese is melted and eggs are completely set.

Cut into wedges. Sprinkle with parsley.

Makes 6 servings.

Patches of Potatoes

Warm up a winter morning with hearty, homey potato cakes.
Serve alongside any egg dish.

6 medium potatoes
1 small onion, finely chopped
2 Tbsp. flour
2 Tbsp. milk
salt and pepper

Peel the potatoes, grate them, and drain them in a colander. In a medium-size bowl, combine potatoes and onion. Stir in the flour and milk to make a thin batter. Add salt and pepper to taste. Form into patties.

Fry patty in a well-oiled, hot skillet. Brown on both sides. Place on paper towels to remove excess oil.

Savory Fried Potatoes

*Large appetites need hearty foods. These fried
potatoes will guarantee no one leaves the table hungry.*

6 slices bacon

1 Tbsp. butter

6 small russet potatoes, diced

1 yellow onion, finely chopped

½ cup chopped red onion

1 green bell pepper, finely
   chopped

1 red bell pepper, finely chopped

2 garlic cloves, minced

salt and pepper

¼ cup shredded Parmesan
   cheese

chopped fresh parsley, for garnish

Makes 4–6 servings.

Cut bacon in 1-inch pieces and fry in a
tall-sided frying pan until crisp. Remove
from pan and set aside, leaving bacon
grease in pan.

Add the butter to the bacon grease and
melt over medium heat. Stir in potatoes,
onions, peppers, and garlic. Cook, stirring
occasionally, until potatoes are tender and
lightly browned. Season to taste with salt
and pepper.

Serve with crumbled bacon sprinkled
over the dish, followed by Parmesan cheese
and parsley.

Campfire Breakfast Skillet

The perfect companion for some great huckleberry pancakes on a fun camping trip.
Any bear would be envious.

½ pound sliced bacon

4 cups peeled and cubed
potatoes

½ cup chopped onion

6 eggs, beaten

1 cup shredded cheddar
cheese

Over the slow-burning coals of a campfire, cook bacon in a cast-iron skillet to desired doneness. Remove bacon from the skillet and set aside. Add the potatoes and onion to the skillet, sautéing until the potatoes are soft, about 10–12 minutes.

Crumble the bacon into the potatoes. Stir in the eggs, cover, and cook until set, about 2 minutes. Sprinkle the cheese over top. Allow cheese to melt before serving.

Breakfast Fried Potatoes

Being good to your family just got a whole lot easier.

---

4 cups diced potatoes

1 cup chopped onion

4 Tbsp. butter

paprika to taste

salt and pepper to taste

Cook potatoes in boiling water for about 4 minutes, until just a bit tender but not cooked soft. Drain off water.

Heat butter over medium heat in a heavy skillet; add potatoes and onions. Fry, stirring occasionally for even cooking and browning. Season to taste.

Makes 4 servings.

omelets

Bacon and Sweet Onion Omelet

Chili Cheese Omelet

Nevada Omelet

Cheese Omelet

Four-Cheese Omelet

Omelet in a Bag

Rainbow Omelet

Oven-Baked Herb Omelet

Colorado Omelet

Hash Brown Omelet

Potato Cheese Omelet

Father's Day Omelet

Sun-Dried Tomato Omelet

Sun-Dried Tomato Omelet, page 54

Omelet in a Bag, page 47

Omelet Tips

As long as you are organized, omelets are among the easiest dishes to pre-pare. Because omelets cook so quickly, be sure to have your fillings ready before cooking the eggs.

Medium-high heat is essential since it sets the eggs quickly, which helps keep them from drying out.

Gently stirring the eggs at the start helps to cook the eggs evenly and gives the omelet a smooth exterior that won't turn out leathery.

If you are making more than one omelet, just use a paper towel to wipe out the skillet between omelets, and adjust the heat if the skillet gets too hot.

Use water instead of milk to thin your egg batter; milk contains fats that will not cook out of your batter. These fats can leave your omelets runny, no matter how long you cook them.

If you are on a cholesterol-restricted diet, there is no need to deprive yourself. Omelets can easily be made from egg substitutes.

Bacon and Sweet Onion Omelet

This is a tasty twist you'll never forget. Onion lovers, rejoice!

2 slices bacon, chopped

1 small sweet yellow onion,
   minced

2 scallions, thinly sliced

4 large eggs

¼ tsp. salt

⅛ tsp. pepper

½ Tbsp. butter

¼ cup shredded cheddar
   cheese

Cook bacon and onion together in a 10-inch nonstick skillet over medium heat until the bacon is crisp and the onion is soft, about 5 minutes. Toss with 2 thinly sliced scallions. Transfer the mixture to a plate lined with paper towels to drain.

Whisk together the eggs, salt, and pepper. Melt the butter in a 10-inch nonstick skillet over medium heat until it just begins to brown, swirling to coat the pan completely.

Add half of the egg mixture to the skillet and stir gently until it just begins to set, about 10 seconds. Gently pull the cooked eggs back from one edge of the skillet and tilt the pan, allowing any uncooked egg to run to the cleared edge of the skillet, until the egg on top is mostly set but still moist, about 2 minutes.

Remove the pan from the heat and sprinkle with half of the cheddar cheese, allowing the cheese to melt. Add half the bacon and onion mixture. Carefully slide half of the omelet onto a warmed plate and, with a firm grip, tilt the skillet slightly so that the remaining half of the omelet folds over the filling. Repeat with remaining egg mixture, bacon-onion mixture, and cheese.

Makes 2 servings.

Chili Cheese Omelet

Flavor is what you will remember with this wonderful egg, bean, and cheese omelet.

½ pound precooked sausage
links

1 (15-oz.) can vegetarian chili
with beans

1¼ cup shredded Mexican
cheese, divided

2 Tbsp. butter or margarine

3 large eggs

4 Tbsp. chopped chives,
divided

sour cream, for garnish

salsa, for garnish

Cut the sausage into small chunks. In a medium-size skillet, brown the sausage over medium-low heat in a medium skillet. When brown, add the chili and stir in ½ cup of cheese. Cook for 3–5 minutes.

Heat an 8-inch skillet over medium-low heat, and melt the butter. By tilting the pan, completely coat the bottom with the butter.

Beat the eggs together with half of the chives, and pour into the pan. Cook until the egg forms a solid yellow circle.

Cover half of the omelet with the chili-sausage mixture, setting aside ¼ cup. Layer with ½ cup of cheese. Fold the omelet over and top with the remaining chili and cheese. Slide the omelet onto a warmed plate and garnish with a large dollop of sour cream, salsa, and the remaining chives.

Makes 2 servings.

Nevada Omelet

South-of-the-border flavor is what you'll get with this omelet.
A nice way to start off a perfect sunny day!

1 Tbsp. butter

¼ cup diced onion

¼ cup diced bell peppers

¼ cup diced, cooked lean ham

4 eggs

2 Tbsp. water

⅛ tsp. salt

dash of pepper

¼ cup diced tomatoes

¼ cup cooked, chopped
  sausage links

¼ cup cooked and crumbled
  bacon

¼ cup diced deli-sliced roast beef

¾ cup finely shredded cheddar
  cheese, divided

In a saucepan on medium-low heat, melt butter. Add onions and bell peppers, cooking until soft. Do not brown.

Stir in diced ham, and cook until the ham is limp and heated through. Remove from heat and set aside.

In a medium bowl, add eggs, water, salt, and pepper; beat and stir with a wire whisk. Set aside.

Heat a frying pan on medium-low heat. Coat with nonstick vegetable spray. Pour egg mixture in pan, and sprinkle with onions, bell pepper, ham, tomato, sausage, bacon, roast beef, and half of the shredded cheese. Cover pan with a lid until omelet starts to set. Remove lid and fold omelet from the sides to the middle, folding in half. Sprinkle with the rest of the cheese.

Cheese Omelet

You'll definitely say cheese when you smile for this breakfast picture!

---

4 eggs
¼ tsp. salt
⅛ tsp. pepper
½ Tbsp. butter
¼ cup shredded cheddar
   cheese

Whisk together the eggs, salt, and pepper. Melt the butter in a 10-inch nonstick skillet over medium heat until it just begins to brown, swirling to coat the pan completely. Add two eggs to the skillet, and stir gently until they just begin to set, about 10 seconds.

Gently pull the cooked eggs back from one edge of the skillet and tilt the pan, allowing any uncooked egg to run to the cleared edge of the skillet. Repeat until the egg on top is mostly set but still moist, about 2 minutes.

Remove the pan from the heat, sprinkle with half of the cheddar cheese, and let it melt. Carefully slide half of the omelet onto a warmed plate, and with a firm grip, tilt the skillet slightly so that the remaining half of the omelet folds over the filling in a half circle. Repeat.

Makes 2 servings.

Four-Cheese Omelet

Have some egg with your cheese! Caution, this omelet is for cheese lovers only.

2 Tbsp. butter, melted

3 eggs, beaten well

2 Tbsp. diced Provolone cheese

2 Tbsp. shredded cheddar cheese

2 Tbsp. diced Swiss cheese

2 Tbsp. diced Monterey Jack

Using an 8-inch nonstick frying pan, melt butter over medium heat. Add well-beaten eggs to prepared pan. As the eggs begin to set, add the four cheeses evenly over the eggs. As the cheeses begin to melt, and before the eggs turn brown, carefully turn egg mixture over. Continue to cook until the cheese melts. Turn omelet 1 more time.

The finished omelet will be a nice yellow color with the cheese melted. Serve immediately.

Omelet in a Bag

Omelets in a Bag is sort of like an arts and crafts project for the breakfast camper. You can make as many as needed or just one if you like. So enjoy a four-star omelet next time you're camping.

1 quart-size resealable freezer
   bag
2 eggs
salt and pepper to taste
optional items: cheese, onions,
   green peppers, ham, tomatoes,
   mushrooms, olives, salsa

Bring a large pot of water to boil.

Crack the eggs into the freezer bag. Add the optional items according to your taste. Take the bag and, with both hands, smash the contents so that the eggs are blended and the fillings are incorporated.

Squeeze out the extra air, seal the bag tightly, write your name on the outside with permanent marker (if making more than one), and drop into the pot of boiling water. Boil for 15 minutes. After removing from boiling water, pour contents onto serving plate.

Tips:

Line a large cup with your plastic bag, folding the top around the lip of the cup for easier filling.

Use a large pot so bags float freely; otherwise the bags could melt when they come in contact with the sides of the hot pot.

Omelets in a bag can be made ahead and frozen to take on camping trips, or refrigerated until needed.

Rainbow Omelet

Short on weekend inspiration?
This delicious omelet has family favorite written all over it!

1 tsp. olive oil

½ red pepper, thinly sliced

½ green pepper, thinly sliced

½ yellow pepper, thinly sliced

4 egg whites

½ tsp. dried basil

¼ tsp. pepper

2 tsp. Parmesan cheese,
   divided

In a large nonstick frying pan over medium heat, warm oil. Add peppers; cook 4–5 minutes, stirring frequently. Keep warm over low heat.

In a small bowl, lightly whisk together the egg whites, basil, and pepper.

Coat a small nonstick frying pan with nonstick cooking spray. Add half of the egg mixture, swirling the pan to evenly coat the bottom.

Cook for 30 seconds or until edges are set. Carefully loosen and flip; cook for 1 minute or until firm.

Sprinkle half of the peppers over the eggs. Fold to enclose the filling. Transfer to plate. Sprinkle with 1 teaspoon Parmesan cheese. Repeat with remaining egg mixture, peppers, and Parmesan cheese.

Makes 2 servings.

Oven-Baked Herb Omelet

The balance of flavor, texture, and spice is nothing less than sensational!

1 clove garlic, minced
2 Tbsp. olive oil
14 basil leaves (8 chopped, 6 for
    garnish)
1 Tbsp. chopped fresh parsley
1 Tbsp. chopped fresh thyme
9 eggs
1 cup milk
salt and pepper to taste
2 Tbsp. shredded Parmesan
    cheese

Preheat oven to 400 degrees. In a small bowl, mix garlic, olive oil, and herbs. In a 2-quart baking dish, bake herb mixture about 10 minutes.

In a separate bowl, beat eggs. Add milk, salt, pepper, and cheese. Pour over herb mixture. Gently mix. Cover with foil, and bake about 30 minutes.

Makes 6 servings.

Colorado Omelet

You'll be amazed at this garden-stuffed omelet that fits into your healthy eating plan!

1 Tbsp. butter

¼ cup diced onion

¼ cup diced bell pepper

¼ cup ham, cooked

4 eggs, beaten

2 Tbsp. water

¼ tsp. salt

¼ cup diced tomato

¼ cup cooked, sliced sausage
   links

¼ cup cooked and crumbled
   bacon

⅓ cup shredded roast beef

¾ cup shredded cheddar
   cheese, divided

In a saucepan over medium heat, melt butter and add onions and peppers. Stir until onions and peppers are soft. Add ham and stir until the ham is limp and heated through. Immediately remove from heat and set aside.

In a mixing bowl, combine eggs, water, and salt. Mix well. Set aside.

Heat a 12-inch frying pan on medium heat. Spray with nonstick spray. Place egg mixture in pan. Sprinkle with onions, peppers, ham, tomato, sausage, bacon, roast beef, and shredded cheese. Cover with lid until omelet starts to set. Immediately remove lid and fold omelet from the sides to the middle. Cook a few seconds more. Serve warm.

Hash Brown Omelet

Perfect for a springtime brunch or even a weeknight dinner,
this quick and simple omelet is jazzed up with the tangy taste of cheddar cheese.

3 cups shredded hash browns
⅓ cup butter, melted
1 cup chopped, cooked ham
1 cup shredded cheddar
   cheese
¼ cup finely chopped green
   pepper
3 eggs, beaten
½ cup milk
½ tsp. salt
¼ tsp. pepper

Makes 6–8 servings.

Preheat oven to 425 degrees.

Press hash browns into bottom and up sides of an ungreased 9-inch pie plate. Drizzle with butter. Bake 25 minutes or until lightly browned. Cool on a wire rack for 10 minutes.

Combine ham, cheese, and green pepper; spoon onto potato shell.

Combine eggs, milk, salt, and pepper, stirring well; pour over cheese mixture.

Lower oven temperature to 350 degrees. Bake 25–30 minutes or until set.

Potato Cheese Omelet

Doubling up on taste can be effortless.
This potato-cheese foldover omelet is proof!

4 slices bacon
2 cups shredded hash browns
¼ cup chopped onion
¼ cup chopped green pepper
4 eggs, beaten
¼ cup milk
½ tsp. salt
dash of pepper
1 cup shredded cheddar cheese

In a medium nonstick skillet, cook bacon until crisp. Remove bacon, crumble, and set aside, reserving bacon drippings in pan.

Add hash browns, onion, and green pepper to drippings. Cook over medium heat, stirring often, for 7–10 minutes or until potatoes are browned and vegetables are tender.

In a bowl, beat eggs, milk, salt, and pepper. Pour over potatoes. Sprinkle with cheese and bacon.

Cover and cook over medium heat 10–15 minutes or until eggs are set. Do not stir. Fold in half. Cook for a few seconds more.

Makes 1 serving.

Father's Day Omelet

Let Dad sleep in and surprise him with this wonderful omelet. It's got all the stuff he likes.

2 Tbsp. butter
½ cup diced onion
½ cup green peppers, diced
½ cup mushrooms, diced
4 eggs
¼ tsp. salt
pepper
½ cup shredded cheddar
   cheese

In a skillet, sauté green peppers, onions, and mushrooms in butter until tender. Remove with a slotted spoon and set aside.

In a small bowl, beat eggs, salt, and pepper. Pour into the skillet. Cook over medium heat. As eggs set, lift edges, letting uncooked portion flow underneath.

When the eggs are set, spoon vegetables and cheese over one side; fold omelet over filling. Cover and let stand until cheese is melted, 1–2 minutes.

Sun-Dried Tomato Omelet

Simply brilliant—this omelet has an Italian flair that will reinvent your morning routine.

2 Tbsp. butter
3 large eggs, beaten
1 Tbsp. water
2 slices fresh mozzarella
    cheese
2 Tbsp. chopped fresh basil
4–5 sun-dried tomatoes, oil-
    packed
salt and pepper

In a nonstick skillet over medium heat, melt 2 tablespoons butter. Whisk eggs and water together. Pour eggs into skillet, and let cook until underside is set and beginning to brown. Put mozzarella cheese, chopped basil, and sun-dried tomatoes on half of the open omelet. Add a dash of salt and pepper.

Fold the empty half of the egg over the filling and cook just until filling is warmed.

Serve with bacon and fresh fruit.

Makes 1 serving.

eggs

Creamy Scrambled Eggs

Poached Eggs

Egg and Herb Scramble with
Garlic Toast

Angel Eggs

Ham-and-Egg Cheese Sauce on Toast

Scrumptious Scramble

Crunchy Fried Eggs

Cheesy Eggs in Tomato Cups

Divine Filled Croissants

Soft-Boiled Eggs

Turkish Eggs

Eggs Benedict

Italian Parmesan Eggs

Poached Eggs on Onion Tartlets

Microwave Eggs Parmesan

Hard-Boiled Eggs

Ham and Eggs

McDuda Breakfast Sandwich

Traditional Scrambled Eggs

Garlic Tomatoes and Eggs

Bacon-Wrapped Baked Eggs

Baked Eggs with Cheese Sauce

McDuda Breakfast Burrito

Eggs Benedict, page 70

McDuda Breakfast Burrito, page 81

Egg Tips

Large eggs are used in recipes unless otherwise noted.

Eggshells are a natural barrier against bacteria and germs; do not use eggs with damaged shells. Inspect eggs carefully before purchasing and again before using.

Never break eggs straight into a mixture or into the pan when cooking. First crack them individually into a small bowl to check that the egg is fresh.

To test the freshness of an egg, do the following test: Drop the egg into cold water; if the egg sinks, it is fresh; if the egg remains suspended in the water, it is about 2 weeks old; if it floats, the egg is not fresh enough to be eaten and needs to be thrown away.

The quality of fresh eggs is indicated by a letter code (AAA, AA, A, B). AAA is the highest quality. The size of eggs (jumbo, extra large, large, medium, small) is determined by their weight per dozen.

To determine if an egg has been hard-boiled, spin it. If it spins smoothly, it is hard-boiled. If it wobbles, it is raw.

Bring eggs to room temperature before using.

Eggs stay fresher longer when stored in the original carton.

For perfectly chopped eggs, place them in an egg slicer and cut through. Carefully turn the egg sideways and slice again.

To separate an egg, crack it open over a bowl and pass the yolk between the two half shells, letting the egg white fall into the bowl, keeping the yolk in the shell.

You can use large nonstick muffin tins in place of custard cups or ramekin cups. Grease generously before using.

Egg Equivalents:

8—10 egg whites = 1 cup
10—14 yolks = 1 cup
4—6 whole eggs = 1 cup
1 extra large egg = 4 Tablespoons
1 large egg = 3¼ Tablespoons
1 medium egg = 3 Tablespoons

Creamy Scrambled Eggs

Scrambled eggs are simply beaten eggs that are fried and—for lack of a better word—scrambled.
This recipe takes scrambling to the next level!

8 eggs
¼ cup milk
1 Tbsp. chopped green onion
¼ tsp. salt
dash of pepper
2 Tbsp. butter
8 ounces cream cheese, cubed
1 tsp. chopped parsley, for
   garnish

In a large bowl, beat together the eggs, milk, green onion, salt, and pepper.

In a large, lightly oiled skillet, heat the butter to sizzling. Pour in the egg mixture. When the egg just begins to set on the bottom, run a spatula underneath, lifting up to allow the uncooked eggs to flow to the bottom of the pan. Sprinkle in the cream cheese pieces. Continue cooking in the standard manner for scrambled eggs.

When the eggs are set, the cheese will be melted. Serve immediately. Garnish with parsley.

Poached Eggs

Fast and versatile with many ways to be served, this is a popular style.
Serve them plain or with a sauce.

1 Tbsp. vinegar
4 eggs

Heat 2–3 inches of water in a medium saucepan over medium heat until almost boiling. Do *not* add salt. Reducing heat if necessary, bring water to a low simmer. Add vinegar.

For each egg, crack into a small cup and carefully slide the egg from the cup into the simmering water. Repeat.

Cook until the whites are set and the centers are still soft. Remove from water with large slotted spoon. Let drain.

Tip: Poached eggs are usually eaten as soon as they are ready, but they can be cooked ahead and kept in cold water in the refrigerator for up to 2 days. To reheat, immerse the poached eggs in a bowl of boiling water for 30 seconds only.

Egg and Herb Scramble with Garlic Toast

Tasty meets healthy with this garden-fresh combination.

12 eggs, beaten
4 ounces cream cheese, cut
   into small pieces
3 Tbsp. chopped chives
1 tsp. dried basil
dash of salt and pepper
2 Tbsp. olive oil
4 medium tomatoes, sliced
8 slices bread
2 Tbsp. minced garlic
4 Tbsp. butter, softened

In a medium-size bowl, whisk eggs, cream cheese, chives, basil, salt, and pepper.

Preheat a large nonstick skillet over medium heat. Add olive oil to the pan. Heat oil, then add egg mixture.

Scramble to desired consistency and serve with a tomato slice per person, seasoned with salt and pepper.

Butter hot toast as usual and spread each piece lightly with small amount of minced garlic. Serve with tomato slices and eggs.

Angel Eggs

No late-morning brunch would be complete with out an Angel Egg.
These make-ahead eggs will make any breakfast buffet fast and easy.

6 eggs, hard-boiled
½ cup mayonnaise
1 Tbsp. mustard
dash of celery salt
dash of pepper
2 Tbsp. cooked and crumbled
   bacon
1 tsp. minced onion

Remove eggshells from boiled eggs. Slice eggs in half lengthwise. Remove yolks and place in a medium bowl. Add mayonnaise, mustard, celery salt, and pepper to egg yolks. Mix until smooth. Mix in bacon and onion.

Place boiled egg whites on a plate. Spoon egg mixture into hollow in egg white.

Makes 6 servings.

Ham-and-Egg Cheese Sauce on Toast

Smooth and filling, this cheesy sauce is packed full of flavor.
This is a great trick for any morning.

¼ cup butter
¼ cup flour
2 cups milk
½ tsp. onion powder
½ tsp. salt
dash of pepper
2 cups shredded cheddar
    cheese
6 hard-boiled eggs, peeled and
    sliced
2 cups cubed ham
1 (4-oz.) can mushrooms,
    drained
4 slices toast

In a saucepan, melt butter, add flour, and stir until smooth. Stir in milk, onion powder, salt, and pepper. Bring to boil and then simmer 1 minute. Add cheese and stir until melted.

Add eggs, ham, and mushrooms; heat through. Serve over hot buttered toast.

Makes 4 servings.

Scrumptious Scramble

Awaken your senses by adding extra-fragrant ingredients to your morning eggs.

1 tsp. olive oil
½ cup diced red onion
1 cup diced tomato
4 eggs
4 egg whites
2 Tbsp. water
1 Tbsp. dill, fresh or dried
salt and pepper to taste

In a nonstick medium-size pan, heat the oil over medium heat. Add the onion and cook for 2 minutes, stirring several times. Add the tomatoes and cook for 1 more minute. Set aside.

In a medium bowl, lightly beat together the whole eggs, egg whites, and water. Pour the egg mixture into the skillet and cook over medium-low heat, stirring frequently, until the eggs are almost set.

Drain excess water from tomato mixture. Stir in dill. Add to eggs. Season with salt and pepper to taste.

Crunchy Fried Eggs

The sooner you serve the egg, the better it will be.
It is best to fry them individually, but you can cook two at a time if you do it carefully.

large eggs
peanut oil

Fill a small, heavy pan two-thirds full of peanut oil. Place over medium heat. Heat to 350 degrees.

Break an egg into a small bowl and gently slide it into the hot oil.

After a few seconds, the egg will begin to fry. If any egg white starts to spread out, use a spoon to lift the egg white back over the egg to maintain a rounded shape.

After 1 minute, carefully turn the egg over so that it cooks evenly on the other side.

After 2 minutes, the egg will be crunchy on the outside and the yolk will still be slightly runny. Lift it out of the oil with a slotted spoon and drain on paper towels. Serve while hot.

Cheesy Eggs in Tomato Cups

This dish is unusually tasty—a fresh tomato filled with egg and cheese,
baked to perfection, and balanced on a muffin.

4 tomatoes
1 Tbsp. olive oil
4 eggs
2 Tbsp. fresh basil
½ cup shredded Parmesan
   cheese
salt and freshly ground pepper
2 English muffins, halved and
   toasted

Preheat oven to 400 degrees.

Slice off the top of each tomato. Scoop out seeds with a spoon, leaving a thick wall. Rub tomatoes inside and out with olive oil and sprinkle insides with salt. Set tomatoes in baking pan; bake 5–7 minutes, until heated.

Carefully break an egg into each tomato. Sprinkle with basil leaves, Parmesan cheese, and pepper.

Return to oven and bake 8–10 minutes, until eggs are set but not firm. With a spatula, transfer each tomato onto a well-toasted English muffin half.

Makes 4 servings.

Divine Filled Croissants

Discover a new spin on a classic.
This recipe will make a believer out of anyone!

4 croissants
4 Tbsp. butter
8 eggs
¼ cup milk
1 tsp. dried basil
½ cup shredded Monterey Jack
   cheese

Preheat oven to 250 degrees. Warm croissants in oven.

Meanwhile, melt butter in a frying pan. Beat together eggs and milk. Pour into pan and scramble until creamy. Add basil to egg mixture; heat through.

Slice croissants about three-quarters of the way through. Fill with scrambled egg mixture, sprinkle with cheese, and stick under the broiler until the cheese is just melted.

Serve with orange slices.

Soft-Boiled Eggs

What a fun way to eat an egg—delicately cooked and served perched in an egg cup.

6 eggs
1 Tbsp. salt
pepper to taste

Bring the eggs, salt, and 2 quarts water to a boil in a medium saucepan over high heat. As soon as the water reaches a boil, remove the eggs from the pot. Cut off the tip of each egg, leaving the rest of the shell on, and nestle upright into an egg cup or small cup lined with paper towels. Sprinkle with pepper.

Tip: The key is to remove the eggs from the water as soon as the first large bubbles begin to break the surface, just before a rolling boil. Close attention is important; eggs can overcook very quickly.

Turkish Eggs

This aromatic dish will win you over.

½ cup butter
1 small onion, diced
1 green pepper, cut in thin strips
    about the size of matchsticks
2 small tomatoes, peeled,
    chopped
8 ounces feta cheese,
    crumbled
10 eggs, beaten
dash of salt and pepper
2 Tbsp. chopped parsley

In a large skillet, melt butter. Cook onion and peppers until soft. Add tomatoes, cheese, and eggs. Stir until eggs are creamy and just cooked through.

Season eggs with salt and pepper to taste. Sprinkle with parsley.

Eggs Benedict

Let the creamy Hollandaise sauce smooth out your morning routine.

Hollandaise sauce:

3 egg yolks

½ cup butter, warm

1½ Tbsp. cold water

1–3 tsp. lemon juice

salt and white pepper to taste

hot red pepper sauce (optional)

Eggs:

4 thick slices ham or Canadian
  bacon, warmed

4 eggs, poached

2 English muffins, split, toasted,
  and buttered

Heat water in bottom of a double boiler. Remove top of double boiler.

In double boiler top bowl, whisk the eggs, butter, water, and lemon juice until it becomes light and frothy. Season with salt, white pepper, and hot sauce.

Place top of double boiler bowl over the simmering water. Continue to whisk until the eggs are thickened, 2–4 minutes; scrape down sides often. Remove the bowl from over the water and whisk until the mixture cools.

Place ham and poached egg on open half of toasted and buttered English muffin. Repeat. Spoon warm sauce over poached egg. Serve immediately.

Makes 2 servings.

Italian Parmesan Eggs

This dish is simple to prepare, yet oh so elegant when served.
It will soon become one of your favorite breakfast dishes.

6 slices Canadian bacon
6 eggs
²/₃ cup whipping cream
dash of dill, fresh or dried
²/₃ cup shredded Parmesan
    cheese

Preheat oven to 350 degrees.

Grease six muffin cups with nonstick cooking spray. Lay one slice of Canadian bacon in bottom of each greased muffin cup. Crack one egg on top of each Canadian bacon slice. Cover each egg with 1 tablespoon whipping cream.

Sprinkle each egg with 1 tablespoon shredded Parmesan cheese and add a dash of dill.

Bake for 10–15 minutes or until edges become slightly brown. Serve immediately.

Makes 6 servings.

Poached Eggs on Onion Tartlets

Plump poached eggs are
perched on an onion tart and adorned with a creamy thyme sauce.

Tart filling:

4 poached eggs

2 large onions

½ cup butter

¾ cup heavy cream

2 thyme leaves and sprigs, for
   garnish

dash of salt and pepper

flour to dust

Tart pie dough:

1¾ cup flour

½ cup + 1 Tbsp. butter, diced

1 medium egg

1 tsp. salt

2 tsp. sugar

3 Tbsp. cold water

Cut the onions into thin slices. Melt the butter in a saucepan over low heat. Add the onions and cook gently for 20 minutes, stirring every 5 minutes. Pour in the cream, add the thyme leaves, and let simmer for another 20 minutes. Season with salt and pepper. Transfer from pan and set aside.

To make tartlets, put the flour in a mound and make a well in the middle. Place the butter, egg, salt, and sugar into the well.

Using your fingertips, mix all the ingredients in the well together. Then gradually draw in the flour little by little.

Mix until all the ingredients are almost mixed and the dough has a slightly sandy texture. Add the cold water and incorporate, using your fingertips.

Knead the dough 2–3 times with the heel of your hand to make it completely smooth. Roll it into a ball and wrap in plastic wrap. Let rest in the refrigerator for 1–2 hours before using.

Preheat the oven to 325 degrees.

Roll out the dough on a floured surface to a ⅛-inch thickness. Using a 4½-inch round pastry or cookie cutter, cut out 4 round pastries and place on a baking sheet. With a fork, poke the top of each tart disk 4–5 times. Spread the onion mixture evenly on top of the disks and bake 25–30 minutes, until bottoms of tartlets are well cooked and crisp.

Warm poached eggs by carefully pouring boiling water over them and letting them stand 30 seconds. Drain well. Put a poached egg on each onion tartlet.

Microwave Eggs Parmesan

Here is a quick microwave breakfast, lunch, or brunch.
Try it for a late-night snack as well.

2 egg whites
1 egg
2 Tbsp. cooked turkey, cubed
1 Tbsp. shredded Parmesan
  cheese
salt and pepper
2 romaine lettuce leaves
1 tomato, sliced

Place 2 egg whites and 1 whole egg in a microwave-safe bowl; beat lightly. Add turkey, Parmesan cheese, and salt and pepper to taste. Whisk with a fork.

Microwave on high 1 minute; stir. Microwave 30 seconds; stir again. (For drier eggs, microwave 30 seconds more.)

On a plate, place lettuce leaves and tomato slices. Spoon eggs onto tomatoes. Sprinkle with additional Parmesan cheese if desired.

Hard-Boiled Eggs

For a quick snack, a garnish, or something extra in a sandwich or salad, keep a supply of hard-boiled eggs on hand. Cook several eggs at once, then refrigerate them, covered, for up to 1 week.

6 eggs

To hard-cook eggs, place them in a saucepan. Add enough water to cover. Bring to a boil, then reduce the heat to a simmer. Cook eggs 15–20 minutes.

To cool the eggs quickly, pour off the hot water and fill the saucepan with ice water. Let stand at least 5 minutes. This will help separate the egg from the shells and make them easier to peel.

Ham and Eggs

The secret to good ham and eggs is top-quality ham and very gentle heat.
This classic dish is so often ruined by overcooking the ham.

2 Tbsp. butter
2 small slices cooked ham
2 eggs
salt and pepper

In a nonstick skillet, melt the butter over low heat. Warm the ham in skillet 1 minute per side, just long enough to warm through.

Break an egg into a bowl and slide it gently onto a slice of ham; repeat with the other egg. Cook gently until the fried eggs are done as you like them.

Slide a spatula under each slice of ham and place the ham and eggs on a plate. Season lightly with salt and pepper.

Makes 2 servings.

McDuda Breakfast Sandwich

These are popular at my house. English muffins are our favorite choice for fried egg sandwiches; however, biscuits, or even buttered toast, work great too!

4 English muffins
4 eggs
4 slices cooked ham or bacon
4 slices American or cheddar
  cheese
salt and pepper
butter

Toast English muffins; butter.

In heated skillet, melt butter, swirling to coat the pan. Add the eggs to the pan, breaking yolks. Sprinkle eggs with salt and pepper. Cook 2 minutes. Turn eggs over, and cook 1 minute more.

Remove the pan from the heat and quickly assemble the sandwiches by layering the fried eggs, cheese, and ham between the toasted muffin halves.

Makes 4 servings.

Tip: If the ham, bacon, or sausage is already very salty, omit the salt.

Because there are multiple components, it can be tricky to put together a batch of hot egg sandwiches. By keeping the English muffins and meat of choice in the oven while the eggs are cooking, you will be able to assemble sandwiches with still-hot ingredients.

Traditional Scrambled Eggs

Allow two eggs per person for an appetizer or light snack,
or three eggs per person for a main course.

2 Tbsp. butter
4–6 eggs
1 Tbsp. milk
salt and pepper

Melt butter in a shallow nonstick pan over medium heat.

Break 4–6 eggs into a bowl; add the milk. Beat very lightly with a fork. Pour the eggs into the pan with the hot, melted butter; stir.

Cook over low heat, stirring gently with a wooden spoon. It will take 3–4 minutes for the eggs to become slightly set. If you prefer firmer, dryer scrambled eggs, cook for an additional 2 minutes.

When the eggs are cooked to your desired firmness, season with salt and pepper.

Serve immediately.

Garlic Tomatoes and Eggs

Perfect for a fresh summer evening meal or light lunch.
Fresh off the vine means great flavor!

20–24 cherry tomatoes
¼ cup olive oil
1 clove garlic, minced
salt and pepper
¼ Tbsp. butter
8 eggs, beaten
2 Tbsp. cream

In a bowl, soak cherry tomatoes in cold water for about 20 minutes to firm up the skins. Drain well.

Preheat oven to 225 degrees. Mix the olive oil and garlic together and toss with tomatoes. Place tomatoes on a rack set over a roasting pan. Sprinkle with salt. Bake 20 minutes.

Melt the butter in a saucepan. Add the beaten eggs; scramble. Add the cream at the end of cooking. Season with salt and pepper. Top with baked tomatoes.

Makes 4 servings.

Bacon-Wrapped Baked Eggs

Want to please some picky palates? Try this bacon wrap.

olive oil

12 eggs

24 slices bacon

12 slices French bread

salt and pepper

3 tomatoes, sliced

Preheat oven to 400 degrees.

Lightly brush a 12-cup muffin tin with olive oil. Line each cup with one slice of bacon around the side and one on the bottom. Crack an egg into each cup. Season with salt and pepper. Bake 12 minutes.

While eggs are baking, lightly toast French bread slices.

Use a butter knife to loosen bacon-wrapped eggs, placing one on each toasted baguette slice. Top with a slice of tomato.

Baked Eggs with Cheese Sauce

If you don't have custard cups, muffin cups work well.

3 Tbsp. margarine

2 Tbsp. flour

1 tsp. dried basil

¼ tsp. salt

⅛ tsp. pepper

1 cup milk

4 eggs

¼ cup shredded mozzarella
    cheese

fresh basil, for garnish

Preheat oven to 350 degrees.

Spray 4 custard cups with nonstick cooking spray.

In a small saucepan, melt the margarine. Stir in the flour, basil, salt, and pepper. Add milk. Cook and stir over medium heat until thick and bubbly. Remove from heat.

Spoon about 2 tablespoons basil sauce into each custard cup. Break each egg into a small bowl and gently pour into the center of a custard cup. Spoon remaining sauce over eggs.

Bake 18–20 minutes or until eggs are set. Sprinkle with cheese and let stand until cheese melts. Garnish with fresh basil.

Makes 4 servings.

McDuda Breakfast Burrito

These handy egg burritos can be made ahead.
Just wrap, grab, and go!

1 pound ground sausage
½ cup chopped yellow onion
1 Tbsp. chopped green peppers
½ cup chopped tomatoes
10–12 flour tortillas
2 cups eggs (about 9 eggs)
10–12 slices American cheese
favorite taco sauce
sour cream, for garnish
salsa, for garnish

Crumble and fry sausage. Remove from heat and drain. Rinse with hot water and allow sausage to drain.

Place drained sausage in frying pan. Add onion, green peppers, and tomatoes. Heat on medium just until sausage and vegetables are heated through, stirring frequently.

Measure 2 cups of eggs and beat. In large frying pan, scramble eggs as usual. Before eggs are completely cooked, stir in ½ cup sausage mixture. When cooked, remove from heat.

In the middle of 1 flour tortilla, place 1 slice of cheese. Top with 1–2 tablespoons of the egg mixture and roll up tortilla.

Microwave just long enough to heat and melt cheese. Serve with your favorite taco sauce.

Garnish with sour cream and salsa.

meats

Spiral Bacon Twists

Sausage Biscuit Braid

Crescent Piglets

Morning BLT

Oven-Baked Bacon

Restaurant-Style Sausage Gravy

Microwave Bacon

Apple-Glazed Canadian Bacon

Kielbasa Kabobs

Restaurant-Style Sausage Gravy, page 91

Meat Tips

Plan ahead and take the bacon out of the refrigerator 30 minutes before cooking. The slices should separate easily.

Older bacon will cook and burn almost twice as fast as fresh bacon.

If you prefer very crispy bacon, choose thinner slices. Pour off the fat as it accumulates in the pan. Use medium to medium-low heat. Cook slowly, turning often. Pricking with a fork will help alleviate any curling problems.

Bacon fat is highly prized for its flavor as a cooking oil. Let oil cool to room temperature. Store in a covered glass container in the refrigerator.

Always thaw frozen sausage before cooking. Fry sausage slowly, turning occasionally.

To grill sausage, place links or patties on a prepared grill with the rack about 8 inches from the heat source. Grill, turning frequently with tongs (a fork will pierce the sausage casing), until thoroughly cooked, 10–15 minutes.

Spiral Bacon Twists

No more boring bacon! These bacon slices will enhance any breakfast table.
Great presentation for any brunch!

12 slices bacon
metal or wooden skewers

Preheat oven to 375 degrees.

Twist each slice of bacon into a tight spiral. Run 2 skewers through the center of the spiral. At each end of the spiral, push skewers through the bacon to hold in place. Repeat until all slices of bacon are used.

Using a broiler pan, lay the twisted skewers down flat. Bake the bacon on the middle rack in the oven for 15 minutes or until crisp.

Remove skewers and transfer bacon to paper towels to drain.

Sausage Biscuit Braid

A great brunch doesn't mean getting up early.
This elegant braid is part of an easy menu that will let you sleep nice and late.

8 ounces ground sausage

¼ cup chopped onion

¼ cup chopped red pepper

1 tsp. minced garlic

4 ounces cream cheese

1 tsp. basil

1 pkg. refrigerator crescent roll
  dough

1 egg, beaten

Preheat oven to 350 degrees.

Sauté sausage, onion, red pepper, and garlic in medium skillet until sausage is done. Drain off grease. Add cream cheese and basil, stirring until cream cheese is completely melted.

On a floured surface, roll out the crescent roll dough, pressing seams together to create a 12x8-inch rectangle.

Spoon meat mixture down the center of the dough lengthwise. Make cuts from dough edges to filling edges at 2-inch intervals along the sides of meat filling.

Alternating sides, fold strips at an angle across meat filling. Fold bottom end toward filling and finish by stretching last strip and tucking under bottom end.

Using both hands, lift braid onto a cookie sheet coated with nonstick cooking spray. Brush with egg wash and bake 12–15 minutes or until golden brown.

Crescent Piglets

Liven up your spring menu with these easy sausage wraps.
They're a kid favorite.

1 pkg. refrigerator crescent roll
   dough
16 precooked sausage links
¼ cup Dijon mustard
¾ cup honey

Preheat oven to 375 degrees.

Unroll crescent dough; divide along perforations into triangles. Cut each triangle in half to form two triangles, totaling 16 pieces. Wrap 1 dough triangle around each sausage link, starting at wide end of dough triangle. Arrange wrapped sausage links on a baking sheet.

Bake at 375 degrees for 15 minutes or until lightly browned.

Combine Dijon mustard and honey. Use for dipping.

Morning BLT

A classic lunch favorite made to order for breakfast.

---

2 slices bacon
1 egg
2 slices whole wheat bread
2 slices tomato
2 pieces lettuce

Fry bacon. Drain off excess fat and pat dry.

Fry egg, breaking the yolk. Cook until done in center.

Toast bread, spread with mayonnaise, and assemble sandwich with bacon, egg, tomato, and lettuce.

Oven-Baked Bacon

The amount of bacon that can be cooked at one time will vary, depending on the size of the bacon slices and the size of your baking sheet. Once you've tried this, you'll never fry bacon again!

1 pound sliced bacon

Heat oven to 400 degrees. Bacon may be placed in oven any time while it is heating.

Arrange the bacon on a rimmed baking sheet and bake until crisp and brown (10–15 minutes), rotating the baking sheet front to back halfway through. Transfer the bacon to paper towels to let the excess fat drain off before serving.

Restaurant-Style Sausage Gravy

Comfort food at its finest.
There is no better way to start off a busy day.

1 pound ground sausage
6 Tbsp. flour
1½ cup water
2¼ cups whole milk
1 tsp. paprika
½ tsp. salt
dash of pepper

Over medium heat, crumble sausage in frying pan, stirring often. Cook sausage until brown.

With slotted spoon, remove sausage from frying pan and reserve pan drippings. The oil and drippings should measure ¼ cup; a little vegetable oil may be added if needed.

Over medium-low heat, add flour to the pan drippings 1 tablespoon at a time. Stir constantly until flour thickens and turns light brown. Add water slowly and stir. After mixture becomes smooth, add milk, paprika, salt, and pepper. Stir until blended. Let gravy simmer, but do not boil; this will curdle the milk. When blended, add sausage. Then mix and simmer until heated through.

Serve with the Baking Powder Biscuits on page 111.

Microwave Bacon

For the times when you only need a few pieces of bacon.

6 slices of bacon

Place pieces of bacon side by side on two
paper towels on a microwave-safe plate.
Cover with two more paper towels. Microwave on high 6–12 minutes.

Apple-Glazed Canadian Bacon

Canadian bacon doesn't splatter like regular bacon strips do, so it's easier for kids to help cook.

1 Tbsp. butter
¼ cup apple jelly
½ tsp. Dijon mustard
8 slices Canadian bacon
pepper

Melt the butter in a large skillet over medium heat. Add the jelly and mustard and whisk just until the jelly melts; do not boil.

Add the bacon slices and cook, turning occasionally with tongs, for 4 minutes. Season with pepper. Serve at once.

Kielbasa Kabobs

Place these kabobs in the oven with baked French toast or a breakfast strata
and you've got everything ready to go at once.

---

2 rings kielbasa sausage

2 cups fresh pineapple chunks

12 (6-inch) wooden skewers

2 Tbsp. orange juice

¼ cup apricot preserves

Preheat oven to 350 degrees.

Line a baking sheet with foil and spray with nonstick cooking spray.

Cut sausage into 1-inch pieces at an angle. Thread skewers, alternating with sausage and pineapple—four pieces of each per skewer. Place skewers in pan.

Mix orange juice and preserves in a small bowl. Brush glaze over kabobs.

Bake about 45 minutes or until kielbasa is browned.

breads

Baking Powder Biscuits, page 111

Orange-Glazed Blueberry Scones, page 99

Bread Tips

Breads with additions like bacon can be heavy, so be careful not to overcook. They are also quite fragile; do not overmix or handle more than necessary.

Flours absorb moisture differently depending on their protein content. When mixed with liquid, certain proteins form gluten, which gives an elastic quality to dough. Gluten provides the framework for dough to rise by stretching and trapping the gas bubbles given off by yeast as it grows.

Liquid turns to steam and helps create texture. Water yields a crusty loaf with dense crumbs, while milk yields rich and tender crumbs and a softer crust.

Sugar activates the yeast to make the dough rise. It also adds flavor, increases tenderness, and helps the crust brown. Granulated sugar is generally used, but molasses, brown sugar, and honey may also be used.

Salt regulates the growth of the yeast. Too much salt can reduce or destroy yeast action. Salt also enhances the flavor and gives a finer texture.

Butter or shortening makes the dough stretch easily and makes the bread tender. It also contributes to flavor and aids in giving bread a longer shelf life.

Eggs aid in gluten development and provide extra nutrients to bread dough. They also add the flavor and golden color desired in sweet dough.

Breakfast in a Cookie Jar

This recipe is fantastic!
Try substituting craisins for the raisins, and sliced almonds for the walnuts.

½ cup vegetable oil
½ cup applesauce
½ cup brown sugar
1 egg
1 Tbsp. vanilla
2 Tbsp. lemon juice
½ cup oat bran
½ cup 7-grain cereal
½ cup flour
½ cup whole wheat flour
1 tsp. baking soda
½ tsp. salt
1 tsp. cinnamon
1 tsp. allspice
½ tsp. cloves
3 cups oats
1 cup raisins
¼ cup chopped walnuts

Preheat oven to 350 degrees.

In a large mixing bowl, beat together oil, applesauce, and brown sugar. Add egg, vanilla, and lemon juice. Beat again.

In large bowl, sift together oat bran, 7-grain cereal, flours, baking soda, salt, and spices. Mix these ingredients with the wet mixture. Stir in oats. Fold in raisins and walnuts.

Place dough on ungreased cookie sheets by the spoonful. Bake 15 minutes or until golden. Remove from cookie sheet for cooling.

Orange-Glazed Blueberry Scones

These scones have a refreshing, soft blueberry taste,
and the simple orange glaze is delightful.

Scones:

2 cups flour

1 Tbsp. baking powder

1 tsp. salt

⅓ cup sugar

¼ cup butter, chilled and cut in
   chunks

¾ cup buttermilk

1 tsp. vanilla

1 egg

1 pint fresh blueberries

Orange glaze:

2 Tbsp. butter

2 cups powdered sugar, sifted

zest and juice from 2 oranges

Preheat oven to 400 degrees.

In a large bowl, sift together flour, baking powder, salt, and sugar; mix thoroughly. Cut in butter using 2 forks. The butter pieces should be coated with flour and resemble crumbs.

In another bowl, mix buttermilk, vanilla, and egg together. Add this to the flour mixture. Mix just to incorporate; do not overmix the dough.

Roll blueberries in flour to coat. This will help prevent the blueberries from sinking to the bottom of the scone when baked. Carefully fold the blueberries into batter.

Turn dough out onto lightly floured surface. Pat and roll dough into an 8-inch circle, leaving the center of the circle thicker. Cut into 12 wedges. On an ungreased baking sheet, place wedges 1 inch apart. Bake scones 15–20 minutes, until golden brown.

While scones are baking, prepare orange glaze. Combine butter, sugar, zest, and juice in a small saucepan. Stirring constantly, cook until butter and sugar are melted and mixture has thickened. Remove from heat and stir vigorously until smooth and slightly cool.

Drizzle glaze over top of scones. Serve warm.

Makes 12 servings.

Corn Pudding with Bacon

A fabulous Thanksgiving favorite, this one is rich, but worth every calorie.

6 slices bacon
1 small onion, diced
2 cups frozen corn, thawed
½ cup soft bread crumbs
2 eggs, beaten
2 cups milk
1 tsp. salt

Preheat oven to 375 degrees. Butter a 2-quart casserole dish.

Fry bacon until crisp. Remove from fat. Drain, reserving fat. Break bacon into pieces.

Sauté onion in 2 tablespoons of the bacon fat until brown.

In a medium bowl, mix corn, bread crumbs, eggs, milk, and salt. Add bacon pieces and onions. Stir, but do not overmix.

Pour mixture into prepared pan. Bake 40 minutes. Serve with butter or honey butter.

Drop Biscuits

Every cook needs a quick and easy drop biscuit recipe to complement a great egg casserole.
Serve with plenty of butter and jam.

2 cups flour
4 tsp. baking powder
½ tsp. salt
4 Tbsp. butter
1 cup milk

Preheat oven to 450 degrees.

In a large bowl, sift together flour, baking powder, and salt. Cut cold butter into the dry ingredients with a fork until mixture resembles small peas. Add milk all at once. Stir dough until just moistened. Drop from a teaspoon onto an ungreased baking sheet.

Bake 12–15 minutes, until lightly browned.

Breakfast Oatmeal Cookies

These oat cookies are great for breakfast on the run, a healthy before-school snack.

¾ cup brown sugar
½ cup margarine
1 egg
1 tsp. vanilla
3 medium-ripe bananas,
    mashed
1 cup flour
⅔ cup whole wheat flour
2 tsp. pumpkin pie spice
½ tsp. baking soda
½ tsp. salt
2 cups oats, uncooked

Preheat oven to 350 degrees.

In a large bowl, mix all ingredients in order. Drop by tablespoons onto ungreased cookie sheet, flattening to ¾-inch thick.

Bake 8–10 minutes. Do not overbake. Remove from cookie sheet and cool on a wire rack.

Banana Nut Muffins with Oatmeal Streusel

Once upon a time we sowed wild oats; now we bake them in muffins.
The streusel topping is worth chasing.

Muffins:

¼ cup walnuts

1½ cup flour

½ cup whole wheat flour

⅔ cup brown sugar

2 tsp. baking powder

¼ tsp. cinnamon

¼ tsp. salt

1 cup mashed ripe banana

¾ cup milk

3 Tbsp. oil

½ tsp. vanilla

1 egg

Streusel:

6 Tbsp. oats

5 Tbsp. flour

2 Tbsp. brown sugar

2 Tbsp. butter, softened

¼ tsp. cinnamon

Preheat oven to 375 degrees.

Toast the walnuts for both the scones and the topping by baking uncovered in an ungreased shallow pan for 6–10 minutes, stirring occasionally, until golden brown.

To prepare the muffins, in large bowl, combine flours, brown sugar, baking powder, cinnamon, and salt. Make a well in the center.

In another bowl, combine bananas, milk, oil, vanilla, and egg. Stir. Add to well in flour mixture. Stir thoroughly. Fold in toasted walnuts.

Spoon batter into 12 greased muffin cups.

To prepare streusel, combine all streusel ingredients. Cut with 2 knives until mixture resembles coarse meal. Sprinkle streusel over batter.

Bake 22 minutes or until a toothpick inserted comes out clean.

Makes 12 muffins.

Whole Wheat Bacon Biscuits

Now that you have all these great egg recipes,
you can make some wonderful biscuits to go with them.

3 slices bacon
1 cup whole wheat flour
1 cup flour
1 Tbsp. baking powder
½ tsp. salt
¼ cup vegetable shortening

Preheat the oven to 425 degrees.

In a medium-size skillet, fry the bacon over medium heat until crisp. Drain on paper towels, reserving 1 tablespoon of the grease. Crumble the bacon and set aside.

In a large mixing bowl, whisk together both flours, baking powder, and salt. Add the shortening and cut it in with a pastry cutter until the mixture is coarse. Add the crumbled bacon and reserved 1 tablespoon bacon grease. Stir until well blended.

Add the milk and stir just until the dough is soft.

Transfer the dough to a lightly floured work surface and knead 4–5 times. Pat out ½ inch thick, and cut out rounds with a 2-inch biscuit cutter.

Arrange the rounds on an ungreased baking sheet about 1 inch apart. Bake 13 minutes or until golden brown.

Lemon Blueberry Cream Scones

Blissfully sweet and a little tart, these lemon scones just say spring.
Invite a friend over and share the sunshine!

Scones:

2 cups flour

¼ cup sugar

3 tsp. baking powder

½ tsp. salt

½ cup dried blueberries

1 tsp. lemon zest

1⅓ cup cream

Icing:

1 cup powdered sugar

2–3 tsp. lemon juice

Preheat oven to 400 degrees.

In a large bowl, mix flour, sugar, baking powder, and salt with a fork. Stir in blueberries and lemon zest. Add cream all at once; stir just until dry ingredients are moistened.

On a floured surface, gently knead dough until smooth. Pat dough out about ¾ inch thick. Cut with a round 2-inch biscuit cutter. Place 2 inches apart on an ungreased cookie sheet.

Bake 12–15 minutes or until light golden brown. Cool 15 minutes.

To make icing, in a small bowl, stir powdered sugar and enough lemon juice to make it smooth and thin enough to drizzle. Drizzle over scones.

Maple Syrup Nut Scones

Liven up a traditional nut scone by adding maple syrup and a crunchy nut topping.

Topping:

3 Tbsp. flour

2 Tbsp. sugar

¼ cup chopped walnuts

2 Tbsp. butter, chilled

Scones:

½ cup chopped walnuts

2 cups flour

2 Tbsp. brown sugar

2 tsp. baking powder

¼ tsp. salt

½ cup butter, firm

⅓ cup maple syrup

1 egg

2 Tbsp. milk

Preheat oven to 350 degrees.

Toast the walnuts for both the scones and the topping by baking uncovered in an ungreased shallow pan for 6–10 minutes, stirring occasionally, until golden brown.

To make topping, in a small bowl, mix flour, sugar, and nuts. Cut in butter, using a fork, until crumbly; set aside.

Increase oven temperature to 400 degrees.

To make scones, in a large bowl, mix flour, brown sugar, baking powder, and salt. Cut in butter, using two forks, until mixture resembles fine crumbs. Add nuts. Stir in maple syrup, egg, and just enough of the milk so dough pulls away from the side of the bowl and starts to form a ball.

Place dough on lightly floured surface; coat with flour by rolling dough into an 8-inch circle on an ungreased cookie sheet. Brush with additional milk. Sprinkle with topping. Cut into 8 wedges, but do not separate.

Bake 15–18 minutes or until golden brown. Immediately remove from cookie sheet; carefully separate wedges. Serve warm with honey butter or a drizzle of maple syrup.

Makes 8 scones.

BYU's Secret Fry Bread

Rumor has it that this is the one. Try it and then decide!

4½ cups water

2 Tbsp. white vinegar

4 Tbsp. baking powder

4 Tbsp. salt

4 Tbsp. powdered milk

7 cups flour

oil for frying

In a large bowl, combine all ingredients except oil. Mix well. Roll dough into small balls. Flatten into disks.

Deep fry one at a time in oil, flipping over with long tongs to brown other side. Drain on paper towels.

Serve with lots of butter, jam, or cinnamon-sugar. For a fun lunch or dinner, serve with chili, cheese, lettuce, and sour cream.

English Muffin Bread

This is an easy yeast bread—no kneading required!
It is especially good toasted!

6 cups flour, divided
2 pkgs. yeast
1 Tbsp. sugar
2 tsp. salt
¼ tsp. baking soda
2 cups milk
½ cup water
cornmeal

Combine 3 cups flour, yeast, sugar, salt, and baking soda.

Heat milk and water until very warm. Add to dry mix; beat well. Stir in remaining flour.

Spoon into two 8x4-inch greased pans sprinkled with cornmeal. Cover. Let rise 45 minutes.

Bake 25 minutes at 400 degrees. Remove from pans immediately.

Creamy Berry Coffee Cake

*Today's forecast—breezy, sumptuous raspberry
and a sunny disposition.*

Cake:

2½ cups flour
¾ cup sugar
¾ cup butter
½ tsp. baking powder
½ tsp. baking soda
¼ tsp. salt
¾ cup sour cream
1 egg
1 tsp. almond extract
1 tsp. vanilla

Filling:

8 ounces cream cheese,
    softened
¼ cup sugar
1 egg
½ cup raspberry jam

Topping:

½ cup sliced almonds

Preheat oven to 350 degrees.

To make the cake, combine flour and sugar in a large bowl. Cut in the butter using a pastry blender until mixture resembles coarse crumbs. Remove 1 cup crumbs and set aside for topping.

To remaining crumb mixture, add baking powder, baking soda, salt, sour cream, egg, almond extract, and vanilla; blend well. Spread batter over bottom and 2 inches up the sides of a greased and floured 9-inch springform pan.

To make the filling, combine cream cheese, sugar, and egg in a small bowl; blend well. Pour over batter in the pan. Carefully spoon jam evenly over filling.

To make the topping, combine 1 cup of the reserved flour mixture and almonds in a small bowl; sprinkle over top.

Bake 55–60 minutes or until cream cheese filling is set and crust is a deep golden brown. Cool 10 minutes. Remove sides of pan. Serve warm or cool.

Makes 12 servings.

Pear-Cranberry Butter Crunch

*Combine the fresh, smooth flavor of the pear with the sweet, tart flavor of cranberries
and you have a combination that will wake up your senses!*

Fruit mixture:
4 ripe pears, peeled, cored, and
 sliced
1 (12-oz.) bag fresh cranberries
⅓ cup sugar
1 tsp. cinnamon
3 Tbsp. flour

Topping:
⅔ cup brown sugar
¾ cup rolled oats
½ cup flour
½ cup butter

Preheat oven to 375 degrees.

To make fruit mixture, combine pear slices, cranberries, sugar, cinnamon, and flour. Place in greased 9x13-inch baking dish.

To make topping, combine brown sugar, oats, and flour in a medium-size mixing bowl. Cut small pieces of butter into oats mixture with a fork.

Sprinkle topping over fruit mixture. Bake 45 minutes. Cut into squares before serving.

Baking Powder Biscuits

Check out the toppings and butters section to top off these masterpiece biscuits.
They go well with sweet or savory spreads.

2 cups flour
4 tsp. baking powder
1 tsp. cream of tartar
2 tsp. sugar
½ tsp. salt
½ cup shortening
⅔ cup milk

In a large mixing bowl, sift together flour, baking powder, cream of tartar, sugar, and salt. Cut in shortening until mixture forms coarse crumbs.

Add milk all at once; stir until dough forms a loose ball. *Do not overmix.* Turn out onto lightly floured surface. Pat or roll dough ½ inch thick. Cut with 2-inch biscuit cutter. Bake on ungreased cookie sheet 10–12 minutes.

Makes 16 biscuits.

Cereal Cookies

These easy-to-take-along cookies will guarantee no one goes hungry in the morning on the run.

½ cup butter
½ cup sugar
1 egg
2 Tbsp. orange juice
    concentrate
1 Tbsp. orange zest
1¼ cup flour
1 tsp. baking powder
½ cup wheat flakes breakfast
    cereal

Preheat oven to 350 degrees.

In a medium bowl, beat together butter, sugar, egg, orange juice, and zest until light and fluffy. Add flour and baking powder, beating until blended. Stir in cereal.

Drop by teaspoonfuls onto an ungreased cookie sheet. Bake 10–12 minutes or until edges are golden. Remove from cookie sheet onto wire rack for cooling.

french toast

Baked Blueberry-Pecan French Toast

Maple Walnut Stuffed French Toast

Double Berry Stuffed French Toast

Outrageous Strawberry French Toast

Ham-Stuffed French Toast

Apple Craisin French Toast

Easy French Toast Sticks

Outrageous Strawberry French Toast, page 119

French Toast Tips

Use shaped cookie cutters to make beautiful French toast shapes. Fun shapes are great for children and adults.

Just for fun, make French toast in a waffle iron.

To freeze, once bread has absorbed all of the egg mixture, place pieces in a single layer on a cookie sheet and freeze until solid. Wrap pieces individually and return to freezer. To serve, place on a lightly greased cookie sheet and bake in a 500-degree oven for 5 minutes on each side. Brush with melted butter before baking, if desired.

Baked Blueberry-Pecan French Toast

Fresh blueberries are on the market from May to September. Generally, the large berries are cultivated varieties and the smaller berries are wild varieties. Look for a dark blue color with a silvery bloom, the best indication of quality. This bloom is a natural, protective, waxy coating. Buy blueberries that are plump, firm, uniform in size, dry, and free from stems or leaves.

French toast:

1 baguette

6 eggs

3 cups milk

1 tsp. vanilla

½ tsp. nutmeg

1 cup brown sugar, divided

1 cup pecans

2 cups blueberries

¼ cup butter, divided

¼ tsp. salt

Blueberry syrup:

1 cup blueberries

½ cup maple syrup

1 Tbsp. lemon juice

Grease a 9x13-inch baking dish. Cut baguette into 20 (1-inch) slices, and arrange in one layer in baking dish.

In a large bowl, whisk together eggs, milk, vanilla, nutmeg, and ¾ cup brown sugar; pour evenly over bread. Refrigerate, covered, overnight.

Preheat oven to 350 degrees.

Spread pecans evenly in a shallow baking pan and toast on middle rack of oven about 8 minutes. Toss pecans in pan with 1 teaspoon melted butter and salt.

Increase temperature to 400 degrees. Sprinkle pecans and blueberries evenly over bread mixture.

In a small saucepan, heat remaining butter, brown sugar, and salt, stirring until melted. Pour butter mixture over bread and bake 20 minutes.

To make blueberry syrup, in a small saucepan, cook blueberries and maple syrup over moderate heat until berries have burst, about 3 minutes. Pour syrup through a strainer into a heat-proof pitcher, and stir in lemon juice. Syrup may be made 1 day ahead and chilled, covered. Reheat syrup before serving.

Maple Walnut Stuffed French Toast

This is surely a taste journey for the senses!

½ cup butter

1¾ cup chopped walnuts

⅓ cup maple syrup

8 eggs

¼ cup milk

1 Tbsp. vanilla

16 slices Texas toast

1 Tbsp. cinnamon

8 ounces cream cheese, softened

powdered sugar to dust

Preheat griddle.

In a saucepan, melt butter. Add walnuts and sauté 3–5 minutes. Add maple syrup and simmer another 5 minutes, stirring to coat all the walnuts. Remove from heat and set aside.

Whisk together eggs, milk, and vanilla. Dip bread into egg mixture to thoroughly coat both sides. Place bread on greased griddle and sprinkle one side with cinnamon. Grill both sides until golden, about 3 minutes each side.

Remove from griddle in pairs, with cinnamon side facing up. Spread a thin layer of cream cheese on each slice of grilled bread. Place 3 tablespoons maple walnut mixture onto one of the cream cheese–coated slices, then place the other slice on top. Cut in half diagonally. Repeat with remaining bread slices.

Serve with maple syrup and a dusting of powdered sugar.

Double Berry Stuffed French Toast

Each bright, vivid piece is full of big blueberry taste.
The simple but delightful sauce tops it off!

French toast:

12 slices of thick bread

2 pkgs. cream cheese, cubed

½ cup blueberries, fresh or
frozen

½ cup raspberries, fresh or
frozen

10 eggs

⅓ cup maple syrup

2 cups milk

Blueberry sauce:

1 cup water

2 Tbsp. cornstarch

1 cup sugar

1 cup blueberries, fresh or
frozen

1 cup raspberries, fresh or
frozen

1 Tbsp. butter

Grease the bottom of a 9x13-inch glass baking dish with nonstick spray.

Cube the bread, removing the crusts. Place half the cubes of bread in the pan. Cube the cream cheese and place on top of the bread. Sprinkle the blueberries and raspberries over the cream cheese. Place the remaining bread on top of the blueberries.

Beat the eggs. Add the maple syrup and the milk. Pour mixture over the bread and cream cheese. Place plastic wrap over dish and refrigerate overnight.

Preheat oven to 350 degrees.

Remove plastic wrap and replace with foil. Bake 30 minutes. Remove the foil and bake 30 minutes more or until puffed and golden. Let stand 10 minutes before cutting.

While the dish is baking, make the blueberry sauce. In a saucepan, heat the water, cornstarch, sugar, and blueberries until mixture thickens. Then add butter and raspberries. Stir. Serve over French toast.

Outrageous Strawberry French Toast

Positively a crowd favorite!
Serve upside down with whipped cream and strawberries!

1 cup brown sugar
1 Tbsp. corn syrup
1 tsp. cinnamon
5 Tbsp. butter
12 slices whole wheat bread
5 eggs
1½ cup milk
1 tsp. vanilla
whipped cream
fresh or frozen strawberries,
   thawed

In a small saucepan over low heat, stir brown sugar, corn syrup, cinnamon, and butter until melted and blended.

Pour mixture into a 9x13-inch pan. Spread evenly on bottom. Top with 6 slices of bread over mixture, squeezing to fit if necessary. Place remaining 6 slices on top of first 6.

Beat eggs with milk and vanilla. Pour over bread. Cover and refrigerate 8 hours or overnight.

Bake in preheated 350-degree oven 45 minutes.

To serve, cut into 8 servings. Flip over onto plate with a spatula, caramelized side up. Serve with whipped cream and strawberries.

Ham-Stuffed French Toast

Mother's Day brunch special.
Let Mom sleep in while the kids and Dad whip up a scrumptious French toast treat.

½ cup cream cheese
8 slices cinnamon raisin bread
16 slices deli ham
4 eggs
¼ cup milk
1 tsp. vanilla
1 Tbsp. sugar
maple syrup

Spread cream cheese onto 4 slices of bread. Top with ham and cover with another slice of bread.

Beat eggs, milk, vanilla, and sugar in a pie plate with fork. Dip sandwiches in egg mixture, turning over to evenly moisten both sides.

Heat a large nonstick skillet over medium heat and spray with cooking spray. Place sandwiches on grill; cook 2 minutes on each side until golden brown. Serve with maple syrup.

Makes 4 servings.

Apple-Craisin French Toast

Pull up a chair for a new twist on a Northwest apple favorite.

1 cup brown sugar
½ cup butter
2 Tbsp. corn syrup
2 apples, peeled and sliced
½ cup craisins
1 loaf French bread, cut into
   1-inch slices
5 eggs
1½ cup milk
1 tsp. vanilla
1 tsp. cinnamon

In a small saucepan, cook brown sugar, butter, and corn syrup until smooth. Pour into a 9x13-inch baking pan. Spread apple slices and craisins over the syrup. Place the bread on top of the apples and craisins.

Beat together eggs, milk, and vanilla. Pour over the bread. Dust top with cinnamon.

Cover and refrigerate overnight. Uncover and bake 45 minutes at 350 degrees. Cut in squares and serve on platter topped with apples, craisins, and syrup from pan.

Easy French Toast Sticks

These French toast sticks are fun to dip in warm maple syrup or a scoop of warm applesauce.

1 Tbsp. butter
3 eggs
½ cup milk
1 tsp. vanilla
4 slices bread, cut lengthwise
   into 4 strips
cinnamon
sugar
maple syrup

Melt butter in skillet.

Mix eggs, milk, and vanilla in bowl. Beat well.

Soak the bread in egg mixture. Brown the soaked bread in skillet. Sprinkle with a little cinnamon and sugar.

Serve with warm maple syrup.

pancakes

Huckleberry Pancakes

Double Coconut Pancakes

Polish Apple Pancakes

Blender Pancakes

Blender Pancakes, page 129

Double Coconut Pancakes, page 127

Pancake Tips

Hot pancakes are better pancakes. Heat the serving plates in the oven on the lowest setting and serve the pancakes on these heated plates. Be careful with these heated plates around small children. Keep extra pancakes warm in the oven.

You can keep leftover batter stored in the refrigerator for several days. If it gets a little thick, revive it with a little milk and ½ teaspoon baking powder for each cup of batter. Do not over stir.

Huckleberry Pancakes

Tart huckleberries are a perfect way to wake you up on any camping trip.
Get up early and pick them fresh!

2 cups flour
⅓ cup sugar
3 tsp. baking powder
½ tsp. salt
2 eggs, beaten
2 Tbsp. oil
1 cup milk
½ cup huckleberries
butter and maple syrup

Mix the flour, sugar, baking powder, and salt in a bowl. Stir in eggs, oil, and milk until mixed. Do not overmix.

Pour ¼ cup batter on lightly oiled skillet. Then add 1 tablespoon huckleberries to each pancake. Cook 2–3 minutes on each side.

Serve hot with butter and maple syrup.

Double Coconut Pancakes

This popular island favorite packs a crunchy taste of coconut in every bite.

1½ cup flour

2 Tbsp. sugar

¼ cup flaked sweetened
  coconut

1 tsp. baking powder

½ tsp. salt

1 (13-oz.) can coconut milk

1 Tbsp. butter, melted

1 egg, beaten

pineapple

Combine flour, sugar, coconut, baking powder, and salt in a large bowl.

In a separate bowl, mix coconut milk, butter, and egg. Add coconut milk mixture to flour mixture, stirring just until smooth.

Pour about ¼ cup batter per pancake onto a hot nonstick griddle. Cook 3 minutes, until tops are covered with bubbles and edges look cooked. Carefully turn pancakes over; cook 2 minutes or until bottoms are lightly browned. Serve with pineapple and bananas.

Makes 12 pancakes.

Polish Apple Pancakes

These pancakes have a unique flavor and texture. They have less flour than traditional pancakes and are not so cake-like. They can be eaten on the go without syrup.

1 cup flour
1 Tbsp. wheat germ
1 Tbsp. sugar
½ tsp. salt
1 egg
1 cup milk
1 Tbsp. vegetable oil
5 medium apples, peeled and
  thinly sliced
powdered sugar

In a bowl, combine flour, wheat germ, sugar, and salt.

In another bowl, lightly beat egg; add milk and oil. Add this mixture to dry ingredients and stir until smooth. Fold in apples.

Pour batter by ½ cupfuls onto a lightly greased hot griddle. Turn when bubbles form. Cook the second side until golden brown and until apples are tender.

Sprinkle with powdered sugar and serve warm.

Blender Pancakes

This one is quick, fast, easy to pour straight from the pitcher, and easy to clean up.
Kid friendly!

1 cup milk

1 cup flour

1 egg

2 Tbsp. vegetable oil

2 tsp. sugar

1 tsp. salt

In a blender, combine milk and flour. Blend approximately 3 minutes. Add the remaining ingredients until batter is smooth. Cook on hot, greased skillet.

waffles

Creamy Raspberry Waffles

Cranberry Waffles with
   Orange-Apricot Syrup

Peanut Butter Banana Waffles

Cinnamon Raisin Waffles

Oatmeal Waffles
   with Strawberry Syrup

Banana Nut Waffles
   with Whipped Banana Topping

Poppy Seed Waffles with Egg Salad

Granola Waffles
   with Blackberry Syrup

Oatmeal Waffles with Strawberry Syrup, page 138

Waffle Tips

The amount of oil or butter in your batter will determine whether or not your waffles will stick to your waffle maker. If you are consistently making waffles that stick, try increasing the oil or butter.

Waffle batter is a tricky character. The batter should be smooth enough to flow freely through the dimples of the waffles plate, but should never be over-mixed. Overmixing turns the flour into gluten, which produces a chewier, less fluffy texture.

Do not open the waffle iron lid prematurely. As a general rule you should always wait until your waffle maker says it's okay. Lifting the lid too soon could cause your waffle to rip.

Creamy Raspberry Waffles

The only thing better than eating fresh raspberries right off the vine
is eating a hot raspberry waffle right off the waffle iron.

Waffles:

1½ cup flour

½ cup oat flour

1 Tbsp. baking powder

½ tsp. baking soda

¼ cup sugar

2 eggs

1½ cup half-and-half

1 tsp. vanilla

¼ cup vegetable oil

1 cup raspberries, fresh or
    frozen

oil for waffle iron

Sauce:

2 cups whipping cream

¼ cup sugar

¼ cup raspberry preserves

1 cup fresh raspberries

Preheat waffle iron.

In a medium-size bowl, sift together flours, baking powder, baking soda, and sugar.

In a large bowl, beat together eggs, half-and-half, vanilla, and oil. Gradually stir in flour mixture. Beat until smooth. Gently fold in raspberries.

Lightly brush hot waffle iron with oil. Pour on enough batter to fill two-thirds of the waffle iron. Cook until crisp and golden brown.

While the waffles are cooking, prepare Creamy Raspberry Sauce. Keep finished waffles warm in an oven preheated to 250 degrees until ready to serve.

To make sauce, in a medium-size saucepan, combine cream and sugar over medium heat. Cook, stirring until small bubbles start to appear around the edges. Reduce heat and stir in raspberry preserves. Simmer 2 minutes. Remove from heat and let stand 3–5 minutes or until sauce thickens. Gently fold in raspberries. Stir until coated. Serve sauce with hot waffles.

Makes 4 waffles and about 2½ cups sauce.

Cranberry Waffles with Orange-Apricot Syrup

This waffle is a warm and wonderful holiday treat.
Discover your own family's traditions or make new ones.

Waffles:

2¼ cups flour

1½ Tbsp. baking powder

¼ tsp. baking soda

½ cup sugar

¼ tsp. salt

2 eggs

½ cup orange juice

1¼ cup buttermilk

1 tsp. vanilla

⅓ cup vegetable oil

1 Tbsp. orange zest

1 cup fresh cranberries

½ cup chopped walnuts

Syrup:

1½ cup apricot preserves

3 Tbsp. orange marmalade

3 Tbsp. orange juice

3 Tbsp. corn syrup

Preheat waffle iron.

In a medium-size bowl, sift together flour, baking powder, baking soda, sugar, and salt.

In a large bowl, beat together eggs, orange juice, buttermilk, vanilla, oil, and orange zest.

Gradually stir in flour mixture. Beat until smooth. Fold cranberries and walnuts into batter. Lightly brush hot waffle iron with oil. Pour on enough batter to fill two-thirds of the waffle iron. Cook until waffles are crisp and golden brown.

While the waffles are cooking, prepare the Orange-Apricot Syrup. Keep waffles warm in a 250-degree oven until ready to serve. Repeat.

To make syrup, in a small saucepan, combine all syrup ingredients over low heat. Cook, stirring, until small bubbles appear around the edges. Simmer 2 minutes. Keep warm until ready to serve.

Makes 4 waffles and about 1½ cup sauce.

Peanut Butter Banana Waffles

These waffles possess a wonderfully unique nutty flavor that seems to come to life with the smooth taste of bananas. Because they stay so moist and fresh, they make a great snack any time of the day.

1¼ cup flour
¾ cup oat flour
1 Tbsp. baking powder
¼ tsp. baking soda
¼ tsp. salt
2 eggs
2 cups buttermilk
¼ cup butter, melted
¼ cup brown sugar
⅓ cup creamy peanut butter
oil for waffle iron
2 cups fresh sliced bananas
powdered sugar

Preheat waffle iron.

In a medium-size bowl, sift together flours, baking powder, baking soda, and salt.

In a large bowl, beat together eggs, buttermilk, butter, brown sugar, and peanut butter. Gradually stir in flour mixture. Beat until smooth.

Lightly brush hot waffle iron with oil. Pour on enough batter to fill two-thirds of the waffle iron. Cook until crisp and golden brown. Keep finished waffles warm in a 250-degree oven until ready to serve.

Serve hot with fresh sliced bananas. Sift powdered sugar over the waffles.

Makes 4 waffles.

Cinnamon Raisin Waffles

This traditional bread recipe becomes a wonderful waffle treat that everyone will love.
With just enough spice and sweetness, it's the raisins that make this waffle exceptionally nice.

2 cups flour
1½ Tbsp. baking powder
½ tsp. baking soda
½ cup + 4 Tbsp. sugar, divided
3 tsp. cinnamon, divided
2 eggs
1¾ cup buttermilk
¼ cup butter, melted
2 Tbsp. maple syrup
1 tsp. vanilla
½ cup raisins
vegetable oil for waffle iron
butter and maple syrup

In a medium-size bowl, sift together flour, baking powder, baking soda, ½ cup sugar, and 1 teaspoon cinnamon.

In a large bowl, beat together eggs, buttermilk, butter, maple syrup, and vanilla. Gradually add flour mixture. Beat until smooth. Stir in raisins.

Lightly brush hot waffle iron with oil. Pour on enough batter to fill two-thirds of the waffle iron. Cook until golden brown. Repeat with remaining batter.

In a small bowl combine remaining 4 tablespoons sugar and 2 teaspoons cinnamon.

Serve waffles hot with melted butter and warmed syrup. Sprinkle cinnamon and sugar mixture over the waffles.

Makes 4 waffles.

Oatmeal Waffles with Strawberry Syrup

This hearty and delicious waffle is a perfect alternative to a boring bowl of oatmeal.
It makes a nice warm treat on a cold winter morning.

Waffles:

2 cups water

1 cup rolled oats, divided

1 cup flour

¾ cup oat flour

1½ Tbsp. baking powder

¼ tsp. baking soda

¼ tsp. salt

2 eggs

⅓ cup plain yogurt

¾ cup milk

½ cup brown sugar

¼ cup butter, melted

vegetable oil for waffle iron

Syrup:

2 cups strawberry preserves

½ cup water

3 Tbsp. light corn syrup

In a medium-size saucepan, bring water to a boil. Stir in ¾ cup oats. Reduce heat and simmer until all the water is absorbed, 4–5 minutes. Set aside.

Preheat waffle iron.

In a medium-size bowl, sift together flours, baking powder, baking soda, and salt.

In a large bowl, beat together eggs, yogurt, milk, brown sugar, and butter. Gradually add flour mixture. Beat until smooth. Stir in cooked oats. Lightly brush hot waffle iron with oil. Pour on enough batter to fill two-thirds of the waffle iron. Batter will be thick. Push batter to the edges with a wooden spoon.

Sprinkle the top of the batter with 1 tablespoon of the remaining uncooked oats. Cook until crisp and golden brown.

While the waffles are cooking, prepare syrup. Keep finished waffles warm in a 250-degree oven until ready to serve. Repeat with the remaining batter and oats.

To make syrup, in a small saucepan, combine all syrup ingredients over low heat. Cook, stirring, until small bubbles appear around the edges. Simmer 2–3 minutes, stirring occasionally. Serve warm. Makes 2 cups.

Poppy Seed Waffles with Egg Salad

Who says you can't improve on a classic?
The waffle makes a fun foundation!

Waffles:

2 cups flour
1 Tbsp. baking powder
½ tsp. baking soda
¼ tsp. salt
2 Tbsp. sugar
2 eggs, separated
2 cups buttermilk
1 tsp. vanilla
2 Tbsp. vegetable oil
2 Tbsp. poppy seeds
vegetable oil for waffle iron

Egg salad:

8 hard-boiled eggs
¾ cup diced celery
3 Tbsp. chopped green onion
1½ Tbsp. mustard
¼ cup mayonnaise
½ tsp. paprika
¼ tsp. salt
¼ tsp. pepper
lettuce leaves
1 tomato, sliced

Preheat waffle iron.

In a medium-size bowl, sift together flour, baking powder, baking soda, salt, and sugar.

In a large bowl, beat together egg yolks, buttermilk, vanilla, and oil. Gradually add flour mixture. Beat until smooth. Stir in poppy seeds.

In a small bowl, whip egg whites until soft peaks form. Fold into batter.

Lightly brush hot waffle iron with oil. Pour enough batter to fill two-thirds of the waffle iron. Cook until crisp and golden brown.

Keep finished waffles warm in a 250-degree oven until ready to serve. Repeat with the remaining batter.

To make egg salad, peel and chop eggs. In a large bowl, use a fork to mix together eggs, celery, green onions, mustard, mayonnaise, paprika, salt, and pepper. Stir until thoroughly blended. Keep refrigerated until ready to serve. Makes about 3 cups.

To serve, place a lettuce leaf on top of each waffle. Place tomato slices and a scoop of egg salad on the lettuce. Makes about 4 waffles.

Granola Waffles with Blackberry Syrup

These light and crunchy waffles are ideal for a nice, hot breakfast, and they are quick to prepare.

Waffles:

1 cup whole wheat flour

1 Tbsp. baking powder

½ tsp. baking soda

2 eggs

¾ cup vanilla yogurt

1½ cup buttermilk

¼ cup honey

1 tsp. molasses

½ cup brown sugar

¼ cup butter, melted

1 cup granola

vegetable oil for waffle iron

Syrup:

1 tsp. cornstarch

½ cup water

1½ cup blackberries

Preheat waffle iron.

In a medium-size bowl, sift together flour, baking powder, and baking soda.

In a large bowl, beat together eggs, yogurt, buttermilk, honey, molasses, brown sugar, and melted butter. Gradually add flour mixture. Beat until smooth. Stir in granola.

Lightly brush hot waffle iron with oil. Pour on enough batter to fill two-thirds of the waffle iron. Cook until crisp and golden brown. While the waffles are cooking, prepare the syrup. Keep finished waffles warm in a 250-degree oven until ready to serve. Repeat with the remaining batter.

To make Blackberry Syrup, combine cornstarch and water in a small bowl. In a small saucepan, combine blackberries and cornstarch mixture over low heat. Cook, stirring, until small bubbles appear around the edges. Makes about 1½ cup.

Serve waffles with melted butter and hot Blackberry Syrup.

Makes 4 servings.

Banana Nut Waffles with Whipped Banana Topping

*When bananas are combined with almonds and walnuts, the flavor is
so good that it's rumored even monkeys will go nuts for these waffles!*

Waffles:

1 cup flour

1 cup oat flour

1½ Tbsp. baking powder

¼ tsp. baking soda

¼ tsp. salt

½ cup sugar

3 ripe bananas

2 eggs

1 tsp. vanilla

¾ cup buttermilk

¼ cup vegetable oil

¼ cup slivered almonds

¼ cup chopped walnuts

vegetable oil for waffle iron

Topping:

4 ripe bananas, sliced

1 tsp. lemon juice

1 cup whipping cream

2 Tbsp. sugar

Preheat waffle iron.

In a large bowl, sift together flours, baking powder, baking soda, salt, and sugar. In a blender, combine bananas, eggs, vanilla, buttermilk, and oil. Process until smooth. Gradually stir banana mixture into flour mixture. Beat until smooth. Stir in almonds and walnuts.

Lightly brush hot waffle iron with oil. Pour on enough batter to fill two-thirds of the waffle iron. Cook until crisp and golden brown. While the waffles are cooking, prepare the topping.

Keep finished waffles warm in a heated 250-degree oven until ready to serve. Repeat with the remaining batter.

To make Whipped Banana Topping, blend banana slices and lemon juice in a blender until smooth. In a medium bowl, whip together cream and sugar until soft peaks form. Fold in banana puree. Makes about 2 cups.

butters & toppings

Wild Raspberry Jam

Vanilla Maple Cream Syrup

Vanilla Sour Cream

Almond Honey Butter

Cinnamon Honey Butter

Honey Blueberry Spread

Honey Butter

Creamy Honey Butter

Peanut Butter Honey

Honey Walnut Spread

Pecan Honey Butter

Strawberry Butter

Hot Cinnamon Applesauce

Blue Ribbon Apple Butter

Slow-Cooked Apple Butter

Wild Raspberry Jam, page 146

Butter Tips

Flavored butter, also referred to as compound butter, is prepared by blending butter with various ingredients such as fresh herbs, minced garlic, chili powder, pepper flakes, grated citrus zest, or an array of spices, fruits, and vegetables.

Flavored butter is commonly used as a condiment, as an addition to sauces, to baste meats and vegetables while they are grilled or broiled, and as topping for seafood, steaks, chicken, or chops.

Flavored butters can be made by hand, with a blender, or by using a food processor.

Butter is easy to store and an attractive addition to any meal. Butters will remain fresh for up to one year when stored properly in the freezer.

Wild Raspberry Jam

Perfection cannot be attained, but there's no reason to stop trying!
Raspberries in the morning come close. This recipe makes ten 8-ounce jars.

3¾ cups fresh raspberries,
   crushed
6½ cups sugar
¼ cup lemon juice
3 ounces liquid pectin

Place crushed berries into a large kettle. Add sugar and lemon juice; stir well. Place over high heat and quickly bring to a boil. Boil hard for 1 minute, stirring constantly. Remove from heat.

Add liquid pectin, stir, and skim off foam with a metal spoon. Immediately fill hot, sterilized 8-ounce jars. Seal and process in a water bath for 5 minutes.

Vanilla Maple Cream Syrup

Blissfully sweet and dreamy smooth!
You'll never go back to just plain maple.

⅓ cup cream cheese
⅓ cup vanilla yogurt
⅓ cup maple syrup

Soften cream cheese in microwave for 15–20 seconds. Add yogurt and stir until well blended. Mix syrup in gradually until smooth.

Makes 1 cup.

Vanilla Sour Cream

This is marvelous with French toast or pancakes!

---

1 cup sour cream
2 Tbsp. powdered sugar
1 tsp. vanilla

Mix all ingredients together and serve.

Makes 1 cup.

Almond Honey Butter

A simple way to add excitement to bread, muffins, or cereal.

4 ounces almond paste
4 Tbsp. butter, softened
½ cup honey

In a small bowl, beat honey and almond paste with an electric mixer. Beat in butter until creamy. Spread on bread, pancakes, or warm cake.

Makes 1 cup.

Cinnamon Honey Butter

You will spoil your family with this butter.
Make ahead and keep plenty on hand—it will be popular!

2 cups butter, softened
¾ cup honey
3 Tbsp. cinnamon

Mix all ingredients and refrigerate.

Makes 3 cups.

Honey Blueberry Spread

Your family and friends will salute you after they have tried this spread.
Eat it up!

½ cup fresh or frozen
   blueberries, thawed
¼ cup honey, divided
½ cup butter, softened

Heat blueberries and 2 tablespoons honey in a small saucepan to boil over medium heat, stirring constantly. Cook 3–4 minutes or until mixture thickens and is reduced by half. Blend in remaining honey and butter.

Serve spread at room temperature. Store in refrigerator, tightly covered.

Makes about 1 cup.

Honey Butter

You might as well double this recipe. It will save you the time later.
Ever so popular, this classic favorite goes well with just about anything.

1 cup butter, softened
½ cup honey

Combine butter and honey with mixer
until mixed.

Makes 1½ cup.

Creamy Honey Butter

Just when you thought a classic couldn't get any better.
Never underestimate the power of butter. Careful now, this might just put butter over the edge!

1 cup butter, softened
1 cup honey
1 cup whipping cream
2 tsp. vanilla

Cream butter with honey. Slowly add whipping cream, beating constantly until mixture is fluffy. Add vanilla. Keep refrigerated.

Makes 3 cups.

Peanut Butter Honey

Simply brilliant! The perfect toast topper—just add sliced bananas.

1 cup butter, softened
1 cup peanut butter
¼ cup honey

In a food processor, beat ingredients together for several minutes.

Makes 2¼ cups.

Honey Walnut Spread

A sweet spread studded with golden walnuts!

1 cup cream cheese
⅓ cup honey
3 Tbsp. ground walnuts

Beat all ingredients together.

Makes 1⅓ cup.

Pecan Honey Butter

Caution, taste buds! Eat at your own risk!

¼ cup honey
1 cup butter, softened
½ cup chopped pecans

Slowly beat the honey into the butter until well blended. Stir in chopped pecans.

Makes 2 cups.

Strawberry Butter

Any biscuit would be honored to be served with this strawberry butter.
Don't deny its day of fame!

1 cup butter, softened
1 cup sliced strawberries
2 tsp. orange zest
2 drops vanilla

Blend all ingredients in blender or food processor until smooth.

Makes 2 cups.

Hot Cinnamon Applesauce

The apple is truly a fruit worth waiting for!
Hot Cinnamon Applesauce is perfect served with muffins or poured over a tall stack of pancakes.

1 (24-oz.) jar applesauce
½ cup brown sugar
½ cup sugar
2 tsp. cinnamon
dash nutmeg
2 Tbsp. butter

Combine and mix all ingredients in a saucepan. Cook over medium heat 4–5 minutes.

Blue Ribbon Apple Butter

We have the ribbon to prove this one is a first prize winner. My friend Patsy ran away with the blue!

16 cups thick apple pulp (about
   6 pounds of apples)
8 cups sugar
1 cup apple cider vinegar
4 tsp. cinnamon
1 tsp. cloves

Core and slice apples, but do not peel. In a large pot, add only enough water to cook apples until soft. Press through a fine sieve and measure. Combine all other ingredients.

Cook in a large roasting pan at 350 degrees for 2 hours, stirring every 30 minutes, or until mixture reaches desired thickness.

Pour into sterilized jars and top with canning lids and rings that have been soaked in warm water. Process in boiling water bath 10 minutes.

Makes 6 pints.

Slow-Cooked Apple Butter

This is a nice hands-off recipe.
It's easy to prepare and turns out great every time.

10–12 cooking apples, chopped
  (14 cups)
2 cups apple juice
3 cups sugar
1½ cup cinnamon
½ tsp. ground cloves

Core and chop unpeeled apples. Combine with apple juice in slow cooker. Add sugar. Cover; cook on high setting for 4 hours or low setting for 10 hours.

Remove apples from slow cooker and put apples into blender; blend on high speed until smooth. Return apples to slow cooker. Add cinnamon and cloves. Cook on low setting for 1 hour or until mixture reaches desired consistency. For very thick apple butter, remove lid while cooking.

Ladle into 6 sterilized half-pint jars, leaving ½ inch headspace. Adjust lids. Process in boiling water bath 10 minutes.

Apple butter will keep several weeks in refrigerator.

Makes 6 half pints.

breakfast drinks

Morning Citrus Punch

Wake-Up Smoothie

Luscious Fruit Smoothie

Banana Yogurt Smoothie

Peach Orange Smoothie

Pink Smoothie Deluxe

Instant Breakfast Smoothie

Frosty Fruit Smoothie

Banana Oatmeal Smoothie

Berry Almond Blast

Summer Morning Delight

Mango Banana Smoothie

Peaches and Dreams Smoothie

Kiwi Dream Smoothie

Apricot Apple Smoothie

Vegetable Smoothie

Peanut Butter Banana Breakfast Drink

Angel Brunch Frost

Wake-Up Smoothie, page 166

Smoothie Tips

Use frozen fruit. The recipes don't always specify, but if you have time, freeze your fruit beforehand; your smoothie will stay colder and be thicker than if your fruit is at room temperature. Large fruits, like bananas or melons, should be chopped into pieces before freezing. Spread the pieces on a plate or baking sheet before freezing. That way they won't freeze into one big lump. Once the fruit is frozen, you can store it in a freezer bag or container.

To keep it healthy, there are lots of small substitutions you can make to lower the fat content of your smoothies. Use skim or soy milk instead of regular milk, or use frozen yogurt instead of ice cream or whole milk. Add nutrition with some wheat germ or protein powder. You can also reduce calories by avoiding sweetened frozen fruit. Use fresh fruit instead.

If your smoothies are coming out thinner than you'd like, add a few more ice cubes to the recipe. Experiment with flavored ice cubes. This is a great way to create a cool and thick smoothie, full of concentrated flavor. To make them, simply pour juice into an ice cube tray and freeze. For a thick, dense smoothie, add an extra handful of frozen fruit, crushed ice, or frozen yogurt.

To grab a smoothie on the go, make it up ahead of time. You can freeze a smoothie and thaw it out when you want it. You'll need to allow some space in the container because your smoothie will likely expand when freezing.

Add the liquids to the blender first, to prevent the blades from getting stuck.

No smoothie is ever better than in the first few minutes after it's made. For the best possible flavor and texture, drink it right away. If you must make them ahead, you'll notice that some smoothies begin to separate after 20 minutes. If that happens, simply stir it or put the smoothie back into the blender for a minute to bring it back to its original consistency.

Morning Citrus Punch

Beautiful citrus color, authentic taste!

---

2 cups water
3 cups sugar
6 cups grapefruit juice
6 cups orange juice
1½ cup lime juice
1 liter ginger ale

In a saucepan, bring sugar and water to a boil; cook 5 minutes. Cover and refrigerate until cool.

Combine juices and sugar mixture; mix well. Just before serving, stir in ginger ale. Serve over ice.

Makes 6 quarts.

Wake-Up Smoothie

For the true smoothie connoisseur, the best of the best!

1 large banana, peeled and
   sliced
½ cup raspberries
1 cup strawberries, hulled
½ cup orange juice
1 cup plain yogurt

Combine all ingredients in blender and
blend until smooth.

Makes 2 smoothies.

Luscious Fruit Smoothie

*Pineapple and mango are blended together to create
an enchanting drink straight from the islands!*

1 (8-oz.) can pineapple chunks
1 large ripe mango, peeled and
    cubed
1 large ripe banana, peeled and
    sliced
1 (8-oz.) carton pineapple
    yogurt
ice cubes

Drain pineapple, reserving juice. Cover
and chill the juice. Freeze fruit.

Combine pineapple juice, frozen fruit,
and pineapple yogurt. Blend until smooth.
With blender running, add ice cubes, one
at a time, to total a fruit-ice mixture of 4
cups. Blend until smooth.

Makes 4 smoothies.

Banana Yogurt Smoothie

Flavored sensation blended with honey!

---

1 (8 oz.) bag frozen mixed
   berries
2 small bananas, peeled, cut
   into pieces, frozen
6 ounces vanilla yogurt
1 cup whole milk
2 Tbsp. honey

Combine all ingredients in blender and
blend until smooth.

Makes 2 smoothies.

Peach Orange Smoothie

Frozen or canned peaches make this smoothie always available, smooth, and delicious!

2 cups peach slices, frozen
3 cups orange juice
1 cup vanilla yogurt, frozen

In a blender, puree peach slices with orange juice. Add frozen yogurt and continue to blend.

You may need to use a rubber spatula to scrape the sides of the blender and free chunks from around the blades.

Add all ingredients to blender and puree until smooth. Pour into glasses and serve immediately.

Makes 4 smoothies.

Pink Smoothie Deluxe

Grapefruit is a popular breakfast fruit. No need to sit down—just pour and go!

1 cup ruby red grapefruit juice
2 cups sliced banana
1½ cup frozen strawberries
1 cup orange juice
1 cup crushed ice

Combine all ingredients in blender and blend until smooth.

Makes 4 smoothies.

Instant Breakfast Smoothie

A great way to take a good instant breakfast and make it even greater!

---

1 cup milk
1 pkg. chocolate instant
   breakfast drink mix
1 Tbsp. peanut butter
1 frozen banana
3 ice cubes

Pour milk into blender. Add remaining ingredients.

Blend until banana and ice are chopped up. Then whip it about 5 seconds.

Makes 1 smoothie.

Frosty Fruit Smoothie

This fresh fruit drink will stick with you all morning long!

1 cup vanilla yogurt
1 cup peaches, sliced
1 banana, cut into chunks
¼ cup wheat germ
¼ cup orange juice
1 cup ice cubes

Combine all ingredients in blender and blend until smooth.

Makes 2 smoothies.

Banana Oatmeal Smoothie

This one is easy to make just about anywhere.
Work or vacation, this breakfast smoothie is a snap!

1 cup milk
1 pkg. plain instant oatmeal
1 banana, cut in chunks
1 cup orange juice

Combine all ingredients in blender and
blend until smooth.

Makes 2 smoothies.

Berry Almond Blast

When berries are at their peak, this breakfast drink is on top of the list for a refreshing pick-you-up!

½ cup blackberries
½ cup raspberries
1 cup milk
¾ tsp. almond extract
2 Tbsp. powdered sugar

Combine all ingredients in blender and blend until smooth.

Makes 1 smoothie.

Summer Morning Delight

This one starts out red, white, and blue, and ends up so good for you!

1 medium banana, peeled and
   sliced
½ cup raspberries
½ cup strawberries
½ cup blueberry yogurt
½ cup crushed ice

Combine all ingredients in blender and
blend until smooth.

Makes 1 smoothie.

Mango Banana Smoothie

Oh baby! Extraordinary made easy.

---

1 (6-oz.) carton pineapple
  yogurt
1 cup milk
1 cup sliced banana
1 cup sliced mango
1 cup crushed ice

In a blender, combine yogurt, milk, banana, and mango. Cover and blend until smooth.

Add ice; cover and blend until smooth.

Makes 2 smoothies.

Peaches and Dreams Smoothie

Summary is here and the time is right!

1¼ cup apple cider
4 slices of peach
3 large strawberries
1 banana
⅛ tsp. cinnamon

Put all ingredients into blender. Blend until smooth.

Makes 2 smoothies.

Kiwi Dream Smoothie

Pretend you're on vacation and you're never coming back!

---

²/₃ cup milk
juice of 2 limes
2 kiwis, peeled and chopped
1 tsp. sugar
2 cups vanilla ice cream

Blend milk, lime juice, sugar, and ice cream until smooth. Then add the kiwis and process until smooth.

Makes 2 smoothies.

Apricot Apple Smoothie

This one's not only great tasting but also good for you.
Simple and nutritious!

4 apricots, pitted
1 cup apple juice
1 apple, peeled, cored, and
   chopped
1 banana, peeled
¾ cup yogurt, plain
1 Tbsp. honey
10 ice cubes

Place all ingredients in a blender and puree until smooth.

Makes 2 smoothies.

Vegetable Smoothie

Here's the perfect New Year's resolution drink!

1 cup plain yogurt
6 ice cubes
1 small cucumber, peeled and
    chopped
1 small tomato
1 chopped celery stalk
3 romaine or spinach leaves
1 Tbsp. minced onion
cucumber slice, for garnish

Puree all ingredients in a blender. Garnish with a cucumber slice.

Makes 1 smoothie.

Peanut Butter Banana Breakfast Drink

Sweet and creamy, peanut butter doesn't always have to be served with jelly.

1 small ripe banana, peeled and
 sliced
2 Tbsp. creamy peanut butter
1 Tbsp. honey
1 cup milk
chopped peanuts, for garnish

Put banana, peanut butter, and honey in a blender. Blend until smooth. Add milk and blend until foamy.

Garnish with chopped peanuts.

Makes 1 smoothie.

Angel Brunch Frost

You'll think you've died and gone to heaven.

---

1 can frozen pink lemonade
   concentrate
1 cup milk
1 (10-oz.) pkg. frozen
   strawberries
1 pint vanilla ice cream
fresh strawberries, for garnish

Place first 4 ingredients in a blender; blend until smooth. Garnish with fresh strawberries.

Makes 4 smoothies.

index

about the author

Carlene Duda attended Ricks College (BYU—Idaho) and Brigham Young University. She is a culinary writer, teacher, and cook.

Her award-winning recipes have been published in newspapers and copyrighted by C&H Sugar Company. *Completely Breakfast* follows her popular *Beyond Oatmeal: 101 Breakfast Recipes.*

Carlene Duda lives in Puyallup, Washington, with her husband, Scott, and their four children.

Photo by Brandy Stone

0 26575 51029 4